Polka-Dot Kids' Quilts

JEAN VAN BOCKEL

Martingale®
& COMPANY

Credits

President · *Nancy J. Martin*
CEO · *Daniel J. Martin*
VP and General Manager · *Tom Wierzbicki*
Publisher · *Jane Hamada*
Editorial Director · *Mary V. Green*
Managing Editor · *Tina Cook*
Technical Editor · *Laurie Bevan*
Copy Editor · *Durby Peterson*
Design Director · *Stan Green*
Illustrator · *Robin Strobel*
Cover Designer · *Regina Girard*
Text Designer · *Trina Craig*
Photographer · *Brent Kane*

That Patchwork Place® is an imprint of Martingale & Company®.

Polka-Dot Kids' Quilts
© 2005 by Jean Van Bockel

Martingale & Company
20205 144th Avenue NE
Woodinville, WA 98072-8478 USA
www.martingale-pub.com

Printed in China
10 09 08 07 06 05   8 7 6 5 4 3 2 1

Mission Statement

Dedicated to providing quality products and service to inspire creativity.

Library of Congress Cataloging-in-Publication Data
Van Bockel, Jean.
 Polka-dot kids' quilts / Jean Van Bockel.
   p. cm.
 ISBN 1-56477-634-4
1. Patchwork—Patterns. 2. Appliqué—Patterns. 3. Quilting.
4. Children's quilts. I. Title.
 TT835.V355 2005
 746.46'041—dc22

                                   2005008701

Dedication

To my parents, George and Audrey White.
I love you, Mom and Dad.

Acknowledgments

With thanks and appreciation to:
 • Pam Mostek, whose helpful and supportive friendship is always present
 • Nona King, for beautiful and timely machine quilting
 • Pat Raffe, who boosted my quilting career
 • The talented Martingale & Company staff, who are so good at making beautiful and informative books

Contents

Introduction · 5

Frosted Animal Cookies · 6

Mini Cookie Quilt · 14

Animal Cookie Onesies · 18

Baby Planets · 20

Circles, Spots, and Polka Dots · 24

Circus Bear · 28

Zippy Quilt · 35

Zoo Polka · 39

Mr. Lucky · 43

Mr. Lucky Pillow · 48

Pocket Quilt · 52

Spotty Dog · 59

Small Pillow · 64

Little Dog Pillowcase · 67

Boxed Dots · 70

Little Dottie · 74

Flannel Blocks with Polka Dots · 77

Naptime Monkey · 81

General Directions · 86

About the Author · 96

Introduction

When my son left for college, I quickly rushed in to claim his closet for more fabric storage space. As I worked my way through his leftover high school papers, favorite books, and sports pictures, I found scrunched in the back corner the old and familiar, worn and faded "nanny," the beloved quilt that had been his comfort and companion for all his childhood years. Seeing that once much-loved treasure brought back a flood of memories of my little boy who is now all grown up. I could see his beloved nanny was much too ragged to pass on to a grandchild, too ugly to donate to the Goodwill, yet too precious to toss away. I realized that this quilt was my son's first prized possession. It was always with him at nighttime, nap time, and for a ride in the car. It was just a very simple little red flannel quilt that my sister made for him when he was born, yet none of us have had the heart to discard it because of the cherished memories that go with it.

That much-loved quilt was the inspiration for the quilts in this book. I've designed them for you to create for the children you love. Not just for those beloved babies, but for their older brothers or sisters too. You'll even find a small pillow and cute pillowcases to match—a perfect present for an older sibling who may be feeling a little left out when a new baby arrives. For a fun project, I've also included directions for a couple of miniature quilts that coordinate with the crib quilts and can be used either for wall decorations or doll quilts.

As you browse through the book, one thing you'll notice is lots and lots of polka dots. Dotted designs are some of my favorite fabrics, and I think they're perfect for children's quilts. They evoke the fun, happy, bright colors that should be in every child's life. The designs for many of the quilts were inspired by important stages in a child's development.

For example, "Circles, Spots, and Polka Dots" on page 24 is designed around the idea that newborns like to focus on strong geometric patterns. "Frosted Animal Cookies" on page 6 is all about textures, from flannel to chenille, and even has tiny pom-poms to represent sugar sprinkles. If you are a beginner, this book is a great place to start. The instructions are simple and easy to follow. I love adding appliqué to my quilts, and the quilts can be stitched either by machine or by hand. There are also some more challenging quilts, such as "Zoo Polka" on page 39 or "Spotty Dog" on page 59, that the intermediate quilter should enjoy. If you need to make a quick donation quilt for an organization, try the "Zippy Quilt" on page 35. Just pick out a colorful polka dot and add some bright solid fabrics for a fast and fun quilt that any child would be pleased to own. You're sure to find a quilt in *Polka-Dot Kids' Quilts* that is just perfect for all the special children in your life.

No matter which delightful quilt you decide to make, you can be certain that it will be overflowing with comfort and love. Whether you are designing a new nursery around your quilt or just making a gift for a baby shower, *Polka-Dot Kids' Quilts* will give you plenty of fun ideas to inspire you and get you on your way to creating a much-loved child's quilt.

Frosted Animal Cookies

Finished quilt size: 38½" x 46½"

Materials

Chenille fabric is most often sold in 50" to 60" widths. The yardage amounts and cutting instructions for the chenille fabric are calculated for a 50" width. If your fabric measures less than this, use the yardage amounts and cutting instructions for the 42"-wide fabric. Flannel tends to shrink a little when washed; the materials list takes this into account.

- ½ yard *each* of 5 flannel fabrics: pink, green, white, blue, and yellow for blocks and appliqué
- ⅜ yard *each* of 4 chenille fabrics (50" wide): pink, blue, purple, and yellow for blocks and borders

  OR ½ yard of *each* color if your fabric is 42" wide
- ½ yard of striped fabric for binding
- 2⅝ yards of flannel for backing
- 44" x 52" piece of batting
- 250 pastel-colored 5-mm pom-poms
- Walking foot (optional, but helpful when sewing with chenille)

Cozy chenille, soft flannel, and baby-sized pom-poms combine to make this the ultimate "feel good" quilt. Tiny fingers will love the soft, comforting textures of the irresistible fabrics.

Designer Tip

The animal shapes are hand appliquéd for a soft, pliable texture so the pom-poms can be easily attached with needle and thread. The pom-poms add a nice bumpy feel to the quilt, but it is important to secure them so they don't get picked off by little fingers and swallowed. Another option would be to use a polka-dot fabric for the animal appliqués and omit the pom-poms.

Cutting

All measurements include ¼"-wide seam allowances.

From *each* of the 5 flannel fabrics, cut:
- 1 strip, 5½" x 42"; crosscut into 4 squares, 5½" x 5½" (20 squares total)
- 1 strip, 3½" x 42"; crosscut into 4 rectangles, 3½" x 5½" (20 rectangles total)

From *each* of the 4 chenille fabrics (50" wide) cut:
- 2 strips, 3½" x 50"; crosscut 1 strip into 5 rectangles, 3½" x 8½" (20 rectangles total)

  OR from *each* of the 4 chenille fabrics (42" wide), cut:
  - 3 strips, 3½" x 42"; crosscut 2 strips into 5 rectangles, 3½" x 8½" (20 rectangles total)

From the striped fabric, cut:
- 5 strips, 2¼" x 42"

Appliquéing the Animal Cookies

1. Trace the pattern shapes on pages 10–13, referring to the directions for freezer-paper or needle-turn appliqué on page 86. Cut four animal shapes from each of the five different leftover flannel fabrics for a total of 20 animals.

2. Center the prepared appliqué shapes on a contrasting 5½" flannel square. Baste or pin in place and appliqué. Make 20 animal squares.

3. To add the pom-poms, thread a needle with a neutral-colored thread. Needle up and down through the animal square and pom-pom four to five times, knotting at the beginning and end. Using a variety of colors, sew 9–14 pom-poms on each animal.

Making the Blocks

1. Sew each appliqué square to a contrasting flannel rectangle as shown. Press the seam toward the rectangle.

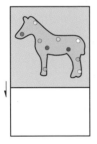

Make 6.

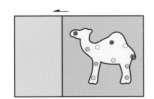

Make 6.

Make 4.

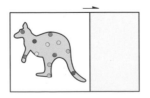

Make 4.

2. Sew a chenille rectangle to each unit from step 1 as shown. To keep the chenille rectangles from shifting while you sew, pin the rectangles in place and use a walking foot. Press the seam toward the flannel fabrics.

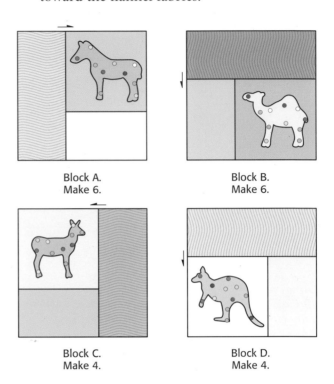

Block A.
Make 6.

Block B.
Make 6.

Block C.
Make 4.

Block D.
Make 4.

Assembling the Quilt

1. Arrange the blocks into five rows of four blocks each as shown below.

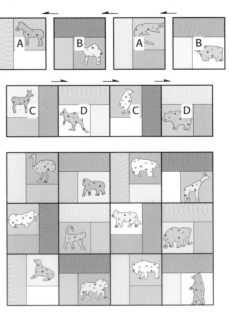

Block layout

2. Sew the blocks together into rows; press the seams in opposite directions from row to row. Sew the rows together and press.

Adding the Borders

Referring to "Straight-Cut Borders" on page 90, add the four remaining 3½"-wide chenille strips to the quilt center.

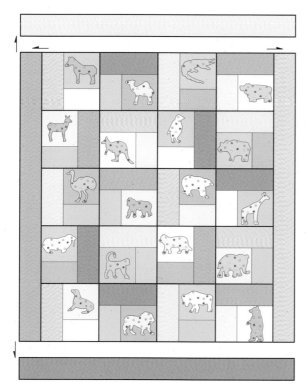

Quilt diagram

Finishing Your Quilt

Refer to "General Directions" on page 86 for specific directions regarding each of the following steps.

1. Layer the quilt top with batting and backing; baste.

2. Machine or hand quilt as desired. My suggestions include quilting in the ditch around the blocks and edge quilting around the appliqués.

3. Trim the batting and backing even with the quilt-top edges.

4. Referring to "Straight-Cut Binding" on page 94, prepare the striped strips for binding and sew the binding to the quilt.

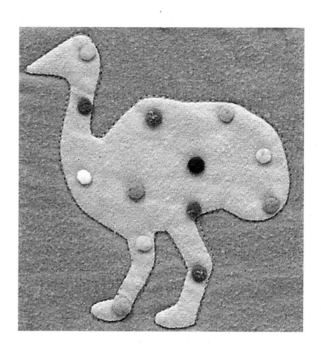

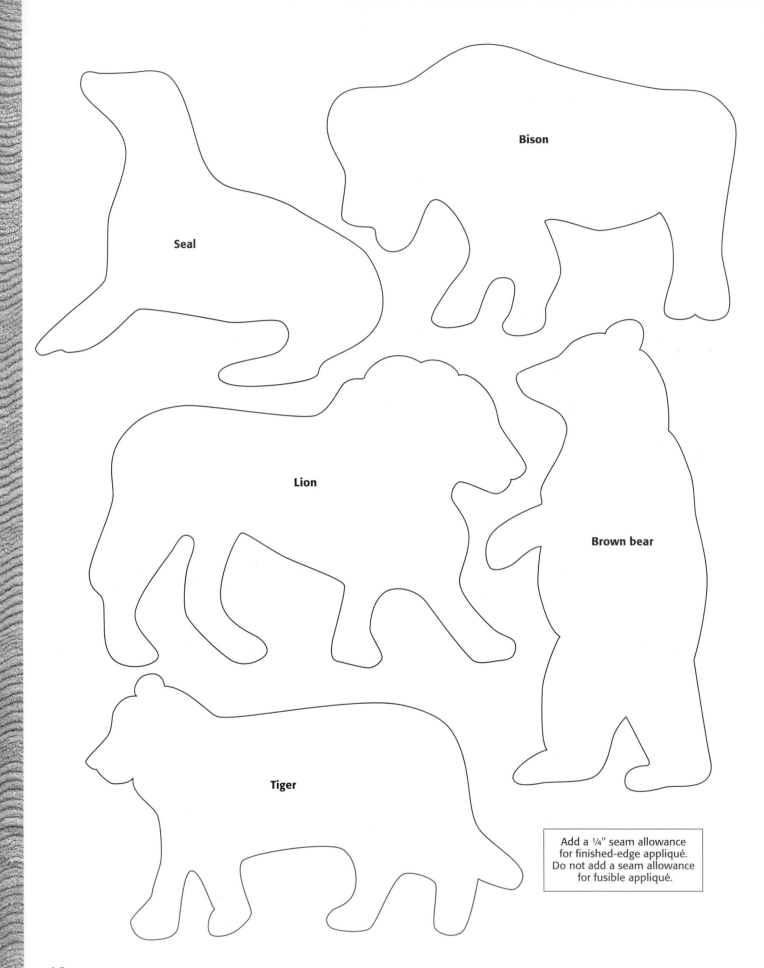

Seal

Bison

Lion

Brown bear

Tiger

Add a ¼" seam allowance
for finished-edge appliqué.
Do not add a seam allowance
for fusible appliqué.

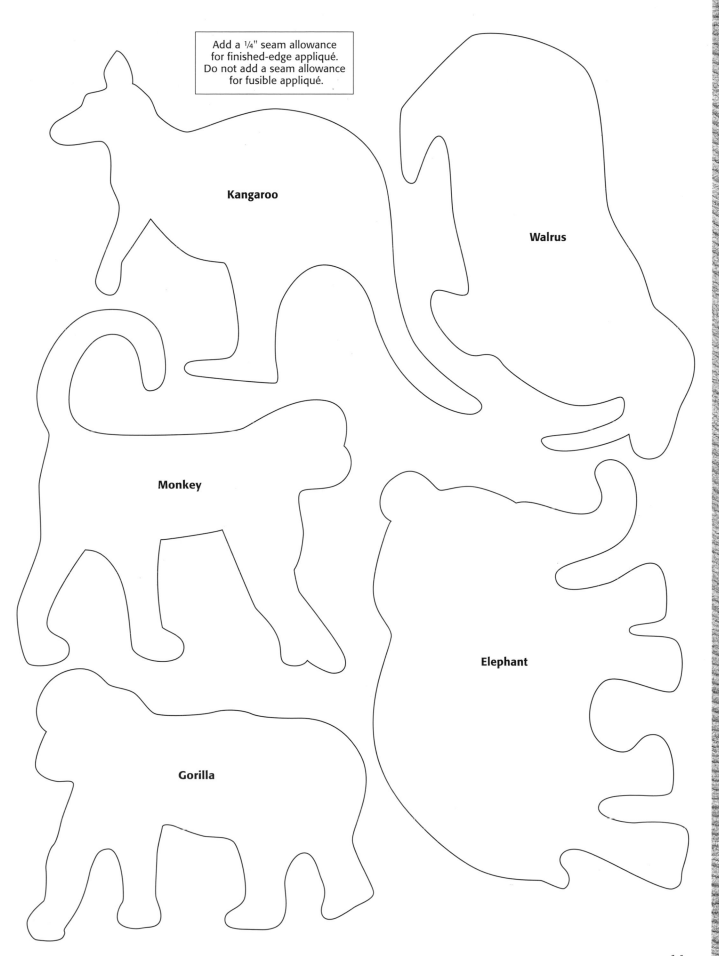

Add a ¼" seam allowance
for finished-edge appliqué.
Do not add a seam allowance
for fusible appliqué.

Kangaroo

Walrus

Monkey

Elephant

Gorilla

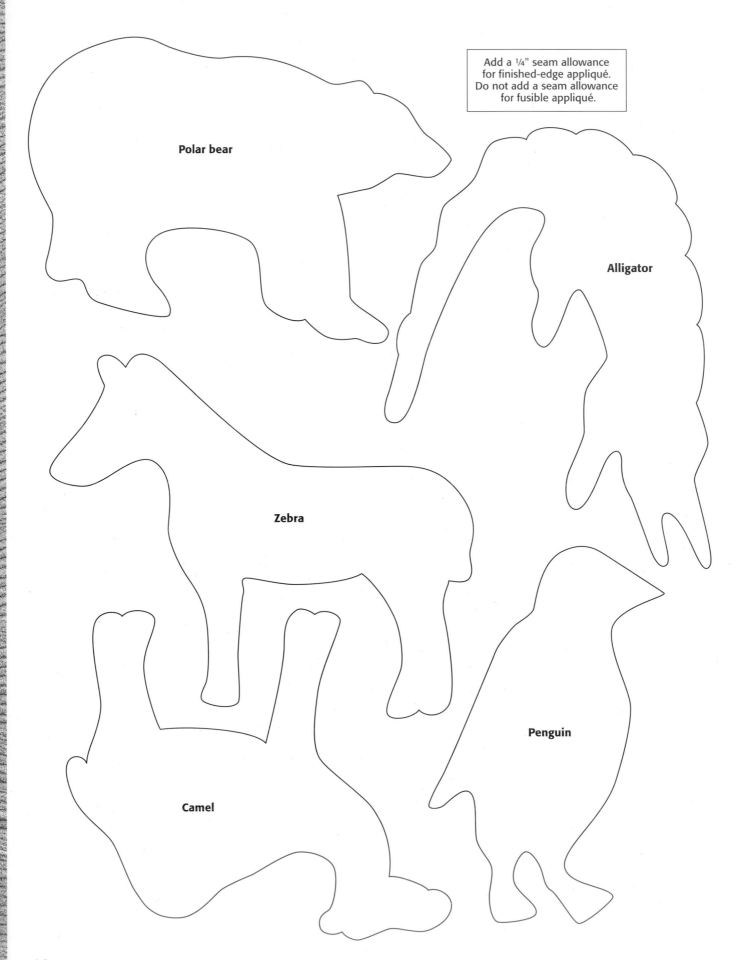

Add a ¼" seam allowance
for finished-edge appliqué.
Do not add a seam allowance
for fusible appliqué.

Polar bear

Alligator

Zebra

Camel

Penguin

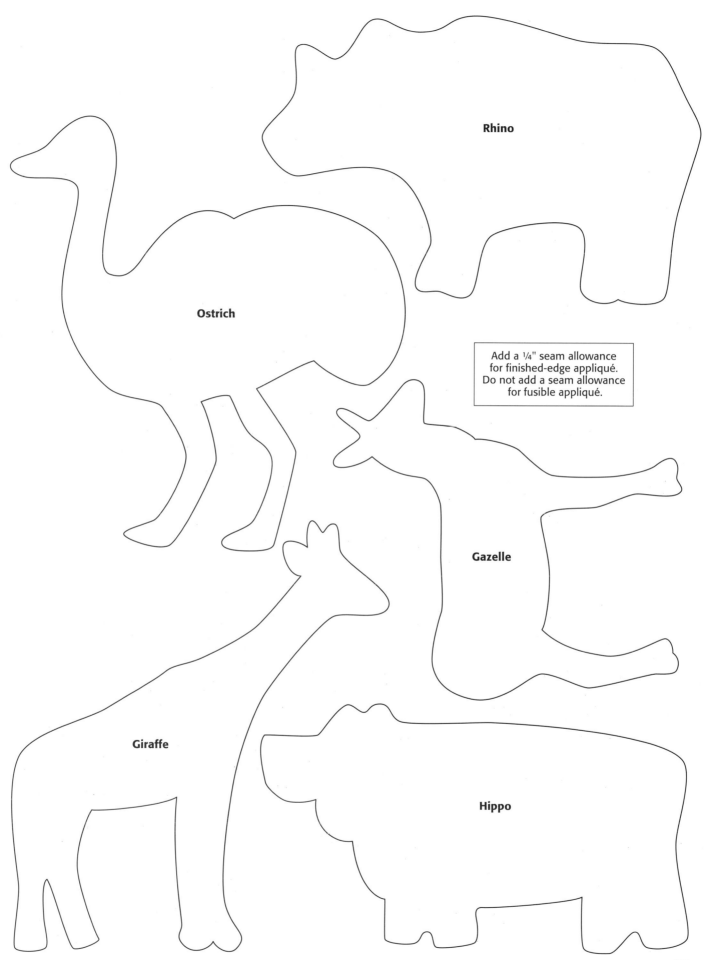

Rhino

Ostrich

Add a ¼" seam allowance
for finished-edge appliqué.
Do not add a seam allowance
for fusible appliqué.

Gazelle

Giraffe

Hippo

Mini Cookie Quilt

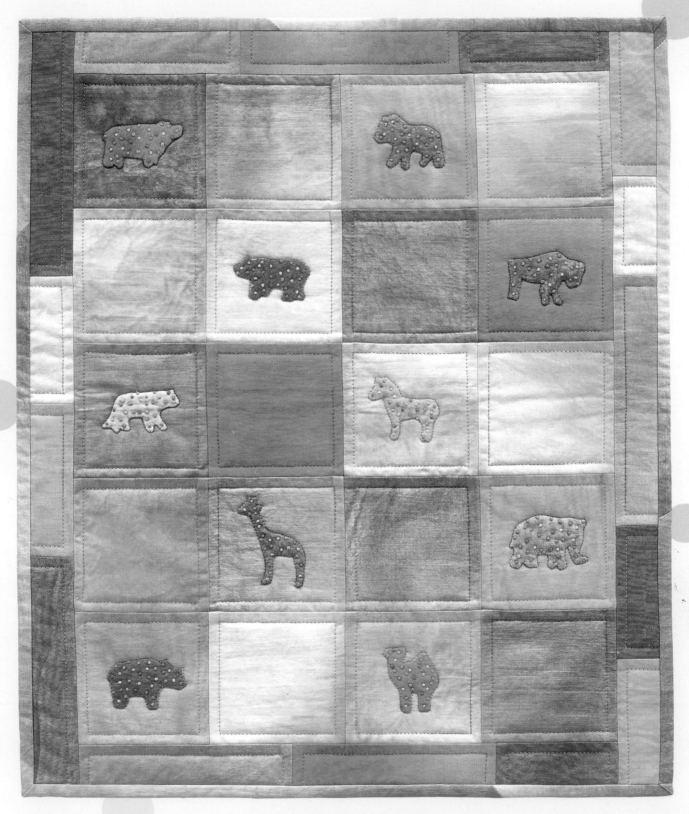

Finished quilt size: 14½" x 17½"

Materials

Yardages are based on 42"-wide fabrics.

- ⅛ yard (or fat eighth) *each* of 8 pastel fabrics: yellow, spring green, teal, aqua, lilac, violet, pink, and blue for blocks, borders, and binding
- ½ yard of backing fabric
- 17" x 20" piece of batting
- Embroidery floss in yellow, pink, teal, purple, and blue
- Pastel variegated thread for quilting

Cutting

All measurements include ¼"-wide seam allowances.

From *each* of the 8 pastel fabrics, cut:

- 3 squares, 3½" x 3½"(24 squares total; you will use 20)
- 1 strip, 1½" x 10" (8 strips total)
- 1 strip, 2" x 10" (8 strips total)

Designer Tip

I used the needle-turn method to appliqué the animal cookies because the cookies are very small. They could also be fused and then machine appliquéd or buttonhole stitched. Just be sure to select a lightweight fusible web so it is easy to add the French-knot sprinkles.

This sweet little doll quilt is perfect for the older brother or sister who will surely be pleased to have a quilt to match the new baby's. I used hand-painted cotton fabrics, but there are many lovely commercial fabrics that will also capture subtle baby hues.

Appliquéing the Animal Cookies

1. Trace the pattern shapes on page 17, referring to the directions for needle-turn or fusible appliqué on pages 86–87. Cut the 10 animal shapes from the eight leftover pastel fabrics, repeating two of the colors.

2. Center the prepared appliqué shapes on contrasting 3½" squares. Baste or pin in place and appliqué. Make 10 animal squares.

3. To add the sprinkles, sew French knots using one strand of embroidery floss. Sew three to four French knots in one color on one animal; then go to another so you are not constantly changing the thread color. Add approximately 15 to 20 sprinkles to each animal.

French knot

Assembling the Blocks

1. Arrange the 3½" squares into five rows of four squares each. Start with an appliqué square and alternate with a plain square. Check the block layout for placement.

2. Sew the blocks together into rows; press the seams in opposite directions from row to row. Sew the rows together and press.

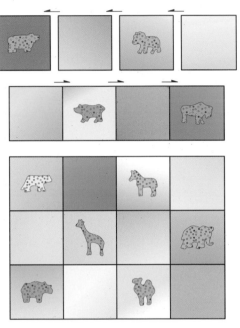

Block layout

Assembling and Adding the Border

1. Sew the 1½"-wide strips end to end, varying the lengths of the strips from 3" to 6", to make two border strips that measure 12½" and two that measure 17½".

2. Sew one 12½"-long border strip to the top and one to the bottom of the quilt. Press the seams toward the border strips. Sew one 17½"-long border strip to each side of the quilt and press the seams toward the border strips.

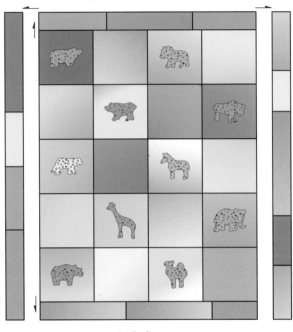

Quilt diagram

Finishing Your Quilt

Refer to "General Directions" on page 86 for specific directions regarding each of the following steps.

1. Layer the quilt top with batting and backing; baste.

2. Machine or hand quilt as desired. My suggestions include quilting in the ditch around the blocks and edge quilting around the appliqués. Stitch ¼" inside the squares using a pastel variegated thread.

3. Trim the batting and backing even with the quilt-top edges.

4. Referring to "Straight-Cut Binding" on page 94, join the 2"-wide strips with diagonal seams, varying the length of the strips from 8" to 10", to make a 74"-long binding strip. Sew the binding to the quilt.

Add a ¼" seam allowance
for finished-edge appliqué.
Do not add a seam allowance
for fusible appliqué.

Animal Cookie Onesies

Materials

- 2 scraps of contrasting fabrics for background and appliqué
- Embroidery floss in yellow, pink, teal, purple, and blue
- Purchased onesie

Cutting

From *each* of the scraps, cut:

- 1 square, 3" x 3" (2 squares total)

Designer Tip

I used the needle-turn method to appliqué the animal-cookie shape because the cookie is very small. It could also be fused and then machine appliquéd. Just be sure to select a lightweight fusible web so it is easy to add the French-knot sprinkles.

Appliquéing the Animal Cookie

1. Trace the animal shape of your choice on page 17, referring to the directions for needle-turn or fusible appliqué on pages 86–87. Cut the animal shape from the 3" square of appliqué fabric.

2. The size of the background rectangle will depend upon which animal shape you have selected. Cut the appropriate-size rectangle from the 3" square of background fabric. For the bear, lion, or tiger, cut a 2" x 2½" rectangle. For the elephant, zebra, buffalo, rhino, or hippo, cut a 2¼" x 2¾" rectangle. For the camel, cut a 2¼" x 2½" rectangle, and for the giraffe, cut a 2½" x 2¾" rectangle.

3. Center the prepared appliqué shape on the background rectangle. Baste or pin in place and appliqué.

When the baby shower is a day away, and the quilt is still in pieces, there is still enough time to create a gift with your own personal touch. Just pick your favorite animal-cookie shape and appliqué it to a purchased onesie for a quick and easy gift.

4. To add the sprinkles, sew French knots using one strand of embroidery floss. Sew three to four French knots using each of the five colors.

French knot

Attaching the Appliqué Patch

1. Turn the edges of the appliqué patch under ¼" and press.

2. Center the patch on the onesie, placing it 1¼" below the neckline. Baste or pin in place and appliqué.

3. Using two strands of embroidery floss, buttonhole stitch around the patch edges.

Buttonhole stitch

Baby Planets

Finished quilt size: 30½" x 40½"

Materials

Yardages are based on 42"-wide fabrics.

- ⅜ yard *each* of 9 assorted soft pastel batik prints for background and binding
- Scraps of aquamarine, lime green, yellow, teal, orange, hot pink, light pink, purple, blue, and violet fabrics for appliqué
- 1½ yards of backing fabric
- 34" x 44" piece of batting

Cutting

All measurements include ¼"-wide seam allowances.

From *each* of the soft pastel batik prints, cut:

- 2 strips, 3½" x 42" (18 strips total); crosscut into lengths varying from 12" to 24"
- 1 strip, 2" x 18" (9 strips total)

Cutting and Arranging the Strips

1. Each row is made up of either two or three 3½"-wide strips that measure a total of at least 42". Cut one vertical row at a time. To cut two adjoining pieces, stack two strips together with right sides up. Align the 45° line of the ruler along the edge of the strips. Cut a 45°

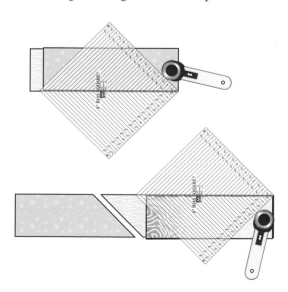

angle on the right end of the strips. Turn the top strip around so that the angles match up. Place another strip on top of the last strip cut. Vary the direction of the diagonal cuts by placing the 45° line of the ruler on the top or bottom fabric edge.

2. Place the rows on your design wall or floor to check color placement and angles. Arrange 10 rows.

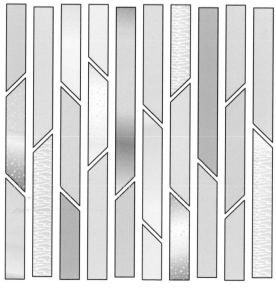

Arrange 10 rows.

Make the baby his or her first piece of art! Luscious batiks blend in the background to give this simple quilt an artistic flare. Use the same yummy color scheme to inspire a creative selection of paint for the nursery walls too.

Sewing the Pieces into Rows

1. With right sides together, sew the pieces together in each row, offsetting the ends of each piece to allow for an accurate ¼" seam allowance. Press the seams in one direction.

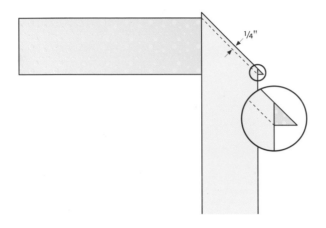

2. Trim each row to measure 40½".

3. Sew the rows together. Press all the seams in the same direction.

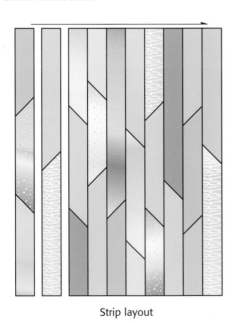

Strip layout

Appliquéing the Circles

The circles for "Baby Planets" were hand appliquéd. You can use your favorite technique. Refer to "Circle Appliqués" on page 89 for detailed instructions.

1. Trace all the circle shapes on page 23 onto template plastic. Write the size of each circle directly on the template.

2. Cut and prepare the circle appliqués as follows: one 4¼" aquamarine circle; one 3½" yellow circle; one 3¼" circle each of aquamarine and orange; one 3" circle each of hot pink, purple, and light pink; one 2¾" circle each of blue and teal, one 2½" circle each of orange, hot pink, and violet; one 2¼" circle of lime green, one 2" circle each of lime green, yellow, and purple.

3. Refer to the quilt diagram for suggested placement of the 16 circles. Baste or pin them in place and appliqué.

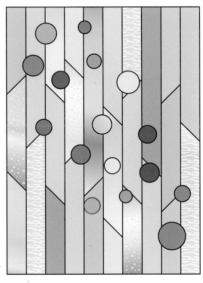

Quilt diagram

Finishing Your Quilt

Refer to "General Directions" on page 86 for specific directions regarding each of the following steps.

1. Layer the quilt top with batting and backing; baste.

2. Hand or machine quilt as desired. My suggestions include quilting circles within circles over the entire piece.

3. Trim the batting and the backing even with the quilt-top edges.

4. Referring to "Straight-Cut Binding" on page 94, prepare the 2"-wide strips for binding and sew the binding to the quilt.

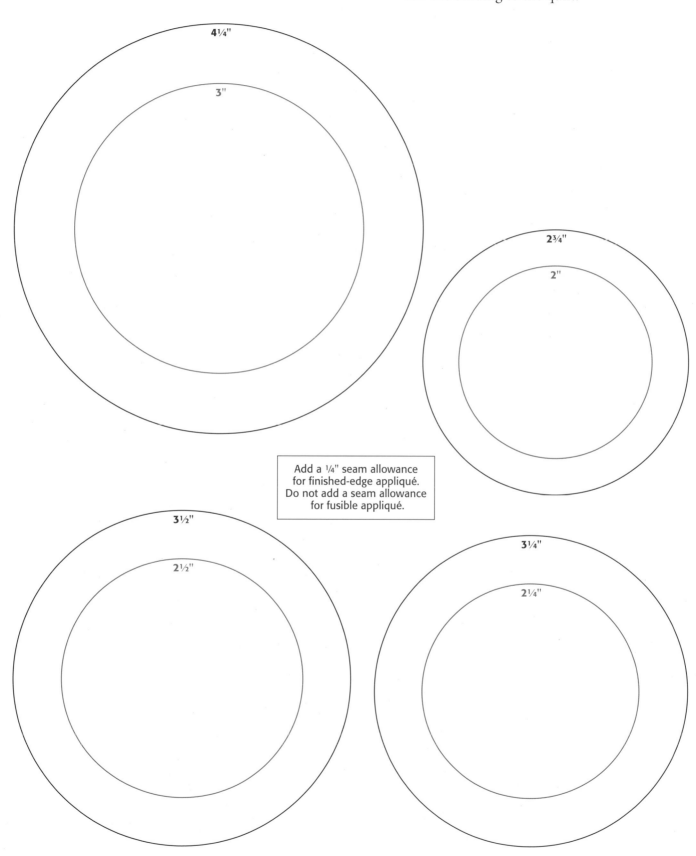

4¼"

3"

2¾"

2"

Add a ¼" seam allowance for finished-edge appliqué. Do not add a seam allowance for fusible appliqué.

3½"

2½"

3¼"

2¼"

Circles, Spots, and Polka Dots

Finished quilt size: 40½" x 48½"

Materials

Yardages are based on 42"-wide fabrics.

- ¼ yard *each* of 5 different red-background polka-dot fabrics for blocks
- ⅜ yard *each* of 3 different white-background polka-dot fabrics for blocks
- ⅝ yard of black-and-white striped fabric for outer border
- ⅝ yard of black fabric for inner border and binding
- ⅜ yard of black-background polka-dot fabric for appliqué
- ¼ yard of black-background with red polka-dot fabric for blocks
- 3 yards of backing fabric
- 46" x 54" piece of batting

Cutting

All measurements include ¼"-wide seam allowances.

From *each* of the 5 red-background polka-dot fabrics, cut:
- 1 strip, 4½" x 42"; crosscut into 7 squares, 4½" x 4½" (35 squares total)

From the black-background with red polka-dot fabric, cut:
- 1 strip, 4½" x 42"; crosscut into 5 squares, 4½" x 4½"

From *each* of the 3 white-background polka-dot fabrics, cut:
- 2 strips, 4½" x 42"; crosscut into 14 squares, 4½" x 4½" (42 squares total; you will use 40)

From the black fabric, cut:
- 5 strips, 1½" x 42"
- 5 strips, 2" x 42"

From the black-and-white striped fabric, cut:
- 5 strips, 3½" x 42"

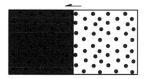

This quilt was inspired by the idea that infants prefer to focus on black-and-white geometric shapes. Black, white, and red make a stunning color impact that can be a nice change from the usual baby colors.

Making the Four Patch Blocks

1. Sew a red or black polka-dot square to a white polka-dot square. Press the seam toward the darker square.

Make 40.

2. Sew the units from step 1 together in pairs as shown. Press 10 seams down and the other 10 seams up. Keep them in separate stacks.

Press 10 seams down.

Press 10 seams up.

Assembling the Quilt

1. Arrange the blocks into five rows of four blocks each. Alternate the blocks from the two stacks so that you will have opposing seams.

2. Sew the blocks together into rows; press the seams in opposite directions from row to row. Sew the rows together and press.

Block layout

Appliquéing the Circles

These circles were machine appliquéd using the invisible-stitch method. You can use your favorite technique. Refer to "Circle Appliqués" on page 89 for detailed instructions.

1. Trace the 3½"-diameter circle on page 23 onto template plastic.

2. Cut and prepare 15 circle appliqués from the black polka-dot fabric.

3. Refer to the quilt diagram on page 27 for suggested placement of the circles. Baste or pin in place and appliqué. For the half circles, use a full circle and place it so it runs off the side of the quilt top. Trim even with the edge of the quilt top after appliquéing.

Trim the circle.

Adding the Borders

1. Sew the black 1½" inner-border strips together end to end. Cut to make two strips that are 45" long and two that are 53" long. Repeat with the striped outer-border strips.

2. Sew each inner-border strip to an outer-border strip of the same length. Press the seams toward the outer-border strips.

3. Referring to "Mitered Borders" on page 91, sew the borders to the quilt top.

Quilt diagram

Finishing Your Quilt

Refer to "General Directions" on page 86 for specific directions regarding each of the following steps.

1. Layer the quilt top with batting and backing; baste.

2. Hand or machine quilt as desired. My suggestions include quilting the blocks in the ditch and quilting around the circles.

3. Trim the batting and backing even with the quilt-top edges.

4. Referring to "Straight-Cut Binding" on page 94, prepare the 2"-wide black strips for binding and sew the binding to quilt.

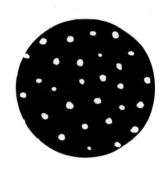

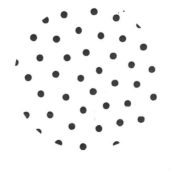

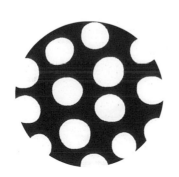

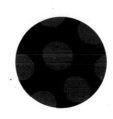

Circus Bear

Finished quilt size: 31½" x 31½"

Materials

Yardages are based on 42"-wide fabrics.

- ¾ yard of black fabric for bear, zigzag border, and binding
- ⅝ yard of black-background polka-dot fabric for patch-ball border, checkerboard border, and outer border
- ⅜ yard of red-background polka-dot fabric for zigzag border
- ¼ yard of white-and-black plaid fabric for patch-ball background
- ¼ yard of white-background polka-dot fabric for checkerboard border
- ⅛ yard of red-and-black polka-dot fabric for center-square border
- ⅛ yard of black-and-white striped fabric for inner accent border
- 9" square of white fabric for center square
- Scraps of assorted polka-dot fabrics with red backgrounds and white backgrounds for balls
- Scrap of black-and-white checked fabric for bear collar
- 1 yard of backing fabric
- 36" x 36" piece of batting
- White embroidery floss

Cutting

All measurements include ¼"-wide seam allowances.

From the red-and-black polka-dot fabric, cut:
- 1 strip, 1½" x 42"; crosscut into:
  - 2 strips, 1½" x 9"
  - 2 strips, 1½" x 11"

From the white-and-black plaid fabric, cut:
- 1 strip, 4" x 42"; crosscut into 8 squares, 4" x 4"

From the black-background polka-dot fabric, cut:
- 1 strip 4" x 42"; crosscut into 8 squares, 4" x 4"
- 4 strips, 2½" x 42"; crosscut into:
  - 2 strips, 2½" x 27½"
  - 2 strips, 2½" x 31½"
- 2 strips, 2" x 42"

From the black-and-white striped fabric, cut:
- 2 strips, ¾" x 42"; crosscut into:
  - 2 strips, ¾" x 18"
  - 2 strips, ¾" x 18½"

From the black fabric, cut:
- 1 strip, 4¼" x 42"; crosscut into 6 squares, 4¼" x 4¼"
- 2 strips, 2⅜" x 42"; crosscut into 26 squares, 2⅜" x 2⅜"
- 1 strip, 2" x 42"; crosscut into:
  - 4 rectangles, 2" x 3½"
  - 4 squares, 2" x 2"
- 4 strips, 2" x 42"

From the red-background polka-dot fabric, cut:
- 1 strip, 4¼" x 42"; crosscut into 6 squares, 4¼" x 4¼"
- 2 strips, 2⅜" x 42"; crosscut into 26 squares, 2⅜" x 2⅜"

From white-background polka-dot fabric, cut:
- 2 strips, 2" x 42"

This quilt is a delightful companion to "Circles, Spots, and Polka Dots." Display this wall hanging by the crib or changing table to capture the attention of its lucky newborn owner. Baby will love its dramatic colors and shapes.

Appliquéing the Center Square

The bear was hand appliquéd using the freezer-paper method, and the balls were also hand appliquéd. You can use your favorite technique. Refer to "Appliquéing" on page 86 and "Circle Appliqués" on page 89 for detailed instructions.

1. Trace the pattern shapes on page 34. Cut the bear shape from the uncut black fabric, the collar from the black-and-white checked fabric, and the ball from one of the polka-dot scraps.

2. Center the prepared appliqué shapes on the 9" white square. Baste or pin in place. Appliqué each piece in numerical order as shown on the patterns.

3. Satin stitch the eye on the bear using two strands of embroidery floss. Stem stitch the eyebrow and ear using one strand of embroidery floss.

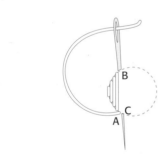

Satin stitch

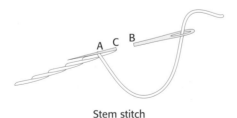

Stem stitch

Adding the Center-Square Border

Sew the 9" red-and-black polka-dot strips to the top and bottom of the center square. Press the seams toward the border strips. Sew the 11" strips to each side and press the seams toward the border strips.

Making and Appliquéing the Patch-Ball Border

1. Each patch ball is cut from a Four Patch block. From the polka-dot scraps, cut 16 squares, 2" x 2". Cut 8 squares with red backgrounds and 8 with white backgrounds. Sew the red squares to the white squares. Press the seam toward the darker fabric. Sew two units together to complete a Four Patch block. Make eight blocks. Press the seams in either direction.

Make 16.

Make 8.

2. The patch balls were hand appliquéd, but you can use your favorite technique. Refer to "Circle Appliqués" on page 89 for more detailed instructions. Trace the circle pattern for the ball onto template plastic. Cut a circle from the center of each Four Patch block for the ball appliqués.

3. Center the prepared ball appliqués on the white-and-black plaid squares. Baste or pin in place and appliqué.

4. Sew a black-background polka-dot square between two ball appliqué squares. Press the seams toward the black-background square.

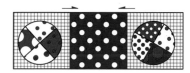

Make 4.

5. Sew a black-background polka-dot square to each end of two units from step 4. Press the seams toward the black-background squares.

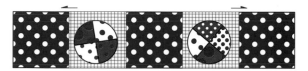

Make 2.

6. Sew the two remaining units from step 4 to the top and bottom of the center square. Press the seams toward the red strip. Sew the units from step 5 to the sides of the center square. Press the seams toward the red strip.

7. Sew the 18" black-and-white striped strips to the top and bottom of the quilt center. Press the seams toward the striped borders. Sew the 18½" strips to each side. Press the seams toward the striped borders.

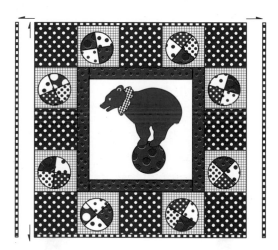

Making the Zigzag Border

1. Following the directions for "Quick and Easy Flying Geese" on page 89, use the 4¼" black squares and 24 of the 2⅜" red-background polka-dot squares to make 24 flying-geese units, 2" x 3½" unfinished.

Make 24.

2. Repeat step 1 using the 4¼" red-background polka-dot squares and the 2⅜" black squares.

Make 24.

3. Pair each flying-geese unit from step 1 with a unit from step 2 and sew them together along the lengths of the rectangles as shown. Press half of the seams toward the top unit and half toward the bottom unit so that the seams abut when you sew the units together in step 4.

Make 24.

4. Sew six units from step 3 together into a row. Make four rows. Press the seams in one direction.

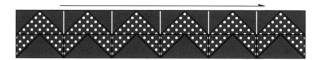

Make 4.

5. Sew two rows from step 4 to the top and bottom of the quilt center. Press the seams toward the striped border. Be sure to position the flying geese as shown.

6. To make the zigzag corners, cut the two remaining 2⅜" red-background polka-dot and black squares diagonally. Sew each red triangle to a black one to make four triangle squares. Press the seams toward the black triangles.

Make 4.

7. Sew the 2" black squares to the triangle squares from step 6. Press the seams toward the black squares. Sew a 2" x 3½" black rectangle to the bottom of each unit. Press the seams toward the rectangles.

Make 4.

8. Sew the corner squares from step 7 to each end of the two remaining rows from step 4 as shown. Press the seams toward the corner squares.

Make 2.

9. Sew these two zigzag rows to both sides of the quilt center. Press the seams toward the striped borders. Once again, be sure to position the flying geese as shown.

Making the Checkerboard Border

1. Sew a 2"-wide white-background polka-dot strip to a 2"-wide black-background polka-dot strip along the length of the strips. Press the seam toward the black fabric. Repeat to make two strip sets. Sew these two strip sets together along the length of the strips, and press the seam in the same direction as the other two seams. Cut this strip set into 17 segments, 2" wide.

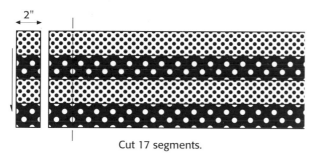

2"

Cut 17 segments.

2. Sew four segments together end to end as shown, and press the seams in one direction.

1 segment

Make 4.

3. Remove the middle seam in the remaining segment. Sew each half to one end of two of the checkerboard strips from step 2.

Remove stitching.

Make 2.

4. Check the quilt diagram for the checkerboard border placement. Sew the short checkerboard strips to the top and bottom of the quilt center. Press the seams toward the checkerboard borders. Sew the longer border strips to the sides of the quilt center. Press the seams toward the checkerboard borders.

Adding the Outer Border

Sew the 27½" black-background polka-dot strips to the top and bottom of the quilt center. Press the seams toward the outer borders. Sew the 31½" black-background polka-dot strips to the sides of the quilt center. Press the seams toward the outer borders.

Quilt diagram

Finishing Your Quilt

Refer to "General Directions" on page 86 for specific directions regarding each of the following steps.

1. Layer the quilt top with batting and backing; baste.

2. Machine or hand quilt as desired. My suggestions include quilting in the ditch and around the outside edges of the appliqués, and stipple quilting the background of the center square.

3. Trim the batting and backing even with the quilt-top edges.

4. Referring to "Straight-Cut Binding" on page 94, prepare the 2"-wide black strips for binding and sew the binding to the quilt.

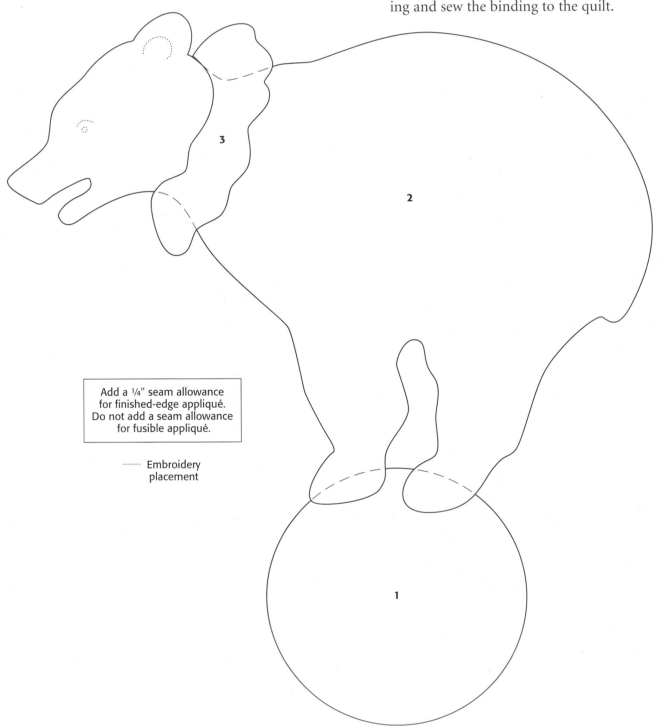

Add a ¼" seam allowance
for finished-edge appliqué.
Do not add a seam allowance
for fusible appliqué.

······· Embroidery
placement

Zippy Quilt

Finished quilt size: 40½" x 52½"

Materials

Yardages are based on 42"-wide fabrics.

- ⅜ yard *each* of orange, yellow, pink, lilac, and plum fabrics for vertical-strip and square rows and binding
- ⅝ yard of white fabric for checkerboard rows and sashing
- ½ yard of polka-dot fabric for triangle-square and on-point rows
- ½ yard of raspberry fabric for vertical-strip and square rows and binding
- ½ yard of purple fabric for vertical-strip and square rows, sashing, and binding
- ½ yard of blue fabric for vertical-strip, square, and on-point rows, and binding
- ⅜ yard of aquamarine fabric for checkerboard and vertical-strip rows and binding
- ⅜ yard of green fabric for vertical-strip rows, sashing, and binding
- 2¾ yards of backing fabric
- 45" x 56" piece of batting

Cutting

All measurements include ¼"-wide seam allowances.

From the raspberry fabric, cut:
- 2 strips, 4⅞" x 42"; crosscut into 10 squares, 4⅞" x 4⅞". Cut each square once diagonally to yield 20 half-square triangles.
- 4 squares, 4½" x 4½"
- 1 strip, 2½" x 20"
- 1 binding strip, 2" x 20"

From the purple fabric, cut:
- 2 strips, 2½" x 40½"
- 2 squares, 4½" x 4½"
- 1 strip, 2½" x 20"
- 1 binding strip, 2" x 20"

This quick-to-do quilt goes together in a snap. Pick a bright, multicolored polka-dot fabric and mix in colorful solids. This one is perfect for those times when you need a quick project for a donation or gift. With sashing strips between each row, there are no seams to match.

From the blue fabric, cut:
- 1 strip, 5¼" x 42"; crosscut into 6 squares, 5¼" x 5¼". Cut each square twice diagonally to yield 24 quarter-square triangles. (You will use 22.)
- 2 squares, 4½" x 4½"
- 1 strip, 2½" x 20"
- 1 binding strip, 2" x 20"

From the aquamarine fabric, cut:
- 3 strips, 2½" x 42"
- 1 strip, 2½" x 20"
- 1 binding strip, 2" x 20"

From the green fabric, cut:
- 2 strips, 2½" x 40½"
- 1 strip, 2½" x 20"
- 1 binding strip, 2" x 20"

From the yellow fabric, cut:
- 4 squares, 4½" x 4½"
- 1 strip, 2½" x 20"
- 1 binding strip, 2" x 20"

From *each* of the orange, pink, lilac, and plum fabrics, cut:
- 2 squares, 4½" x 4½" (8 squares total)
- 1 strip, 2½" x 20" (4 strips total)
- 1 binding strip, 2" x 20" (4 strips total)

From the polka-dot fabric, cut:

- 2 strips, 4⅞" x 42"; crosscut into 10 squares, 4⅞" x 4⅞". Cut each square once diagonally to yield 20 half-square triangles.
- 1 strip, 3⅞" x 42"; crosscut into 10 squares, 3⅞" x 3⅞"

From the white fabric, cut:

- 7 strips, 2½" x 42"; trim 4 strips to 40½" long

Making the Vertical-Strip Rows

The vertical-strip rows in the featured quilt were made with 21 pieces of fabric. However, to simplify the math, I have given instructions for these rows to be made with 20 pieces.

1. From the 2½" x 20" strips of 10 assorted colors, make two strip sets with 5 strips each. Press the seams in one direction. Cut each strip set into four segments, 4½" wide.

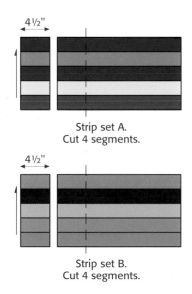

Strip set A.
Cut 4 segments.

Strip set B.
Cut 4 segments.

2. Sew four segments from step 1 together end to end, alternating between A and B segments. Press the seams in one direction.

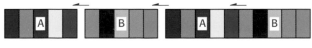

Make 2.

Making the Triangle-Square Rows

1. Sew each raspberry triangle to a polka-dot triangle. Press the seams toward the raspberry triangles.

Make 20.

2. Sew 10 squares from step 1 together as shown to make a row that's 40½" long. Repeat to make a total of two rows.

Make 2.

Making the Checkerboard Rows

1. Sew each 42" aquamarine strip to a 42" white strip along the length of the strip. Press the seams toward the aquamarine strips. Make a total of three strip sets. Cut the strip sets into 40 segments, 2½" wide.

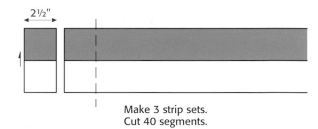

Make 3 strip sets.
Cut 40 segments.

2. Sew 20 segments from step 1 into a checkerboard row, 40½" long. Press all the seams in the same direction. Repeat to make a total of two rows.

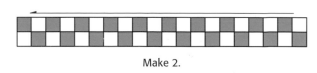

Make 2.

Making the Square Rows

From the 4½" assorted-color squares, sew 10 squares together side to side to make a strip that's 40½" long. Press all the seams in the same direction. Repeat to make a total of two rows.

Make 2.

Making the Polka-Dot On-Point Row

1. Sew a blue quarter-square triangle to each side of a 3⅞" polka-dot square as shown. Press the seams toward the blue triangles.

Make 10.

2. Sew the units from step 1 together as shown. Sew a triangle to each end. Press all the seams in the same direction. Be careful not to stretch your row when pressing.

Add a triangle to each end.

3. Trim the end triangles to a straight edge, leaving a ¼" seam allowance.

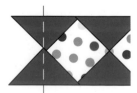 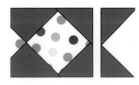

Trim, leaving a ¼" seam allowance.

Assembling the Rows

Sew the pieced rows together with a 40½" white, purple, or green sashing strip between each row. Refer to the quilt diagram for the sashing placement. Press the seams toward the sashing strips.

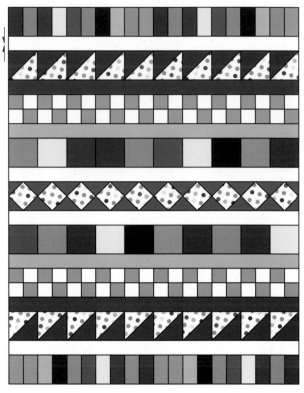

Quilt diagram

Finishing Your Quilt

Refer to "General Directions" on page 86 for specific directions regarding each of the following steps.

1. Layer the quilt top with the batting and backing; baste.

2. Hand or machine quilt as desired. My suggestions include quilting in the ditch and quilting circles, squares, and zigzags in accent thread.

3. Trim the batting and backing even with the quilt-top edges.

4. Referring to "Straight-Cut Binding" on page 94, prepare the assorted 2"-wide strips for binding and sew the binding to the quilt.

Zoo Polka

Finished quilt size: 41½" x 43½"

Materials

Yardages are based on 42"-wide fabrics.

- 1⅝ yards of white fabric for blocks and appliqué strips
- ¼ yard or fat quarter *each* of blue, green, red, and yellow polka-dot fabrics for appliqué
- ⅞ yard of blue large-scale polka-dot fabric for outer border and binding
- ¾ yard of yellow fabric for blocks and inner border
- 1 fat quarter *each* of blue, green, and red fabrics for blocks
- 2¾ yards of backing fabric
- 46" x 48" piece of batting
- ¾ yard of lightweight fusible web

Cutting

All measurements include ¼"-wide seam allowances.

From the white fabric, cut:
- 4 strips, 5½" x 33½"
- 4 rectangles, 14" x 17"

From *each* of the blue, green, and red fabrics, cut:
- 1 rectangle, 14" x 17" (3 rectangles total)

From the yellow fabric, cut:
- 5 strips, 1½" x 42"
- 1 rectangle, 14" x 17"

From the blue large-scale polka-dot fabric, cut:
- 5 strips, 3½" x 42"
- 5 strips, 2" x 42"

Making the Pinwheel Blocks

1. To make the triangle-square units for the Pinwheel blocks, use a pencil or water-soluble marker to draw a grid with five rows of six squares, 2⅜" x 2⅜", on the wrong side of the four white rectangles. The grid should measure 11⅞" x 14¼". Leave no space between the squares and rows as shown. Draw a diagonal line through each square. Place each white rectangle right sides together with a blue, red, yellow, and green rectangle. Pin the layers together between the diagonal lines. Sew ¼" from both sides of each diagonal line as shown.

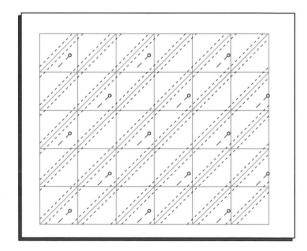

2. Cut along each diagonal, vertical and horizontal line. This will yield 60 triangle-square units from each of the combinations; you will use 55 of each color. Press the seams away from

This quilt is sure to be a favorite—and you'll be surprised by how quickly your favorite youngster can name all the animals. Machine appliqué helps speed up the construction of this very kid-friendly quilt.

the white triangles and trim the extended corners.

Trim.

3. Sew a red triangle square to a green triangle square; then sew a blue triangle square to a yellow triangle square. Press the seams away from the white triangle.

Make 55.   Make 55.

4. Sew the red/green units to the blue/yellow units as shown. Before pressing, remove the vertical stitches in the seam allowances on both sides of each unit. Then press the seam allowances in opposite directions. Where the eight points meet in the middle, press the seams open so the unit makes a tiny pinwheel.

Remove stitches in seam allowance.

Press half of the seam up and half down.

Make 55.

5. Sew 11 pinwheel blocks into a row. Press the seams in one direction.

Make 5 rows.

Appliquéing the Animals

The animals for "Zoo Polka" were fused and machine appliquéd. Refer to "Fusible Appliqué" on page 87 for detailed instructions.

1. Trace the 20 different animal shapes on pages 10–13.

2. From each of the four polka-dot fabrics, cut and prepare five different animal shapes. Refer to the block layout below if you want to exactly match the colors in the project quilt.

3. Evenly space five of the animal appliqués on a 5½" x 33½" white strip. Refer to the block layout if you want to exactly match the animal placement in the project quilt. Iron to fuse in place. Repeat to make three more animal strips.

4. Appliqué the edges of the pieces using a small, tight zigzag stitch; match the top thread with the polka-dot fabric.

Assembling the Quilt

Referring to the block layout, sew the animal appliqué strips between the five pinwheel strips. Press the seams toward the appliqué strips.

Block layout

Adding the Borders

1. Sew the yellow inner-border strips together end to end. Cut to make two strips that are 46" long and two that are 48" long. Repeat with the 3½"-wide blue large-scale polka-dot outer-border strips.

2. Sew each inner-border strip to an outer-border strip of the same length. Press the seams toward the outer-border strips.

3. Referring to "Mitered Borders" on page 91, sew the borders to the quilt top.

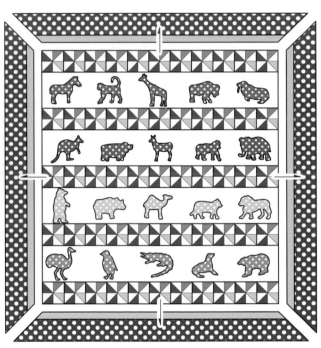

Quilt diagram

Finishing Your Quilt

Refer to "General Directions" on page 86 for specific directions regarding each of the following steps.

1. Layer the quilt top with batting and backing; baste.

2. Hand or machine quilt as desired. My suggestions include quilting in the ditch and stipple quilting around the appliqués.

3. Trim the batting and backing even with the quilt-top edges.

4. Referring to "Straight-Cut Binding" on page 94, prepare the 2"-wide blue large-scale polka-dot strips for binding and sew the binding to the quilt.

Mr. Lucky

Finished quilt size: 40½" x 51". Quilted by Nona King.

Materials

Yardages are based on 42"-wide fabrics.

- 1½ yards of medium green checked fabric for setting triangles and middle border
- ¾ yard of light green fabric for Cat block backgrounds
- ¾ yard of red small-scale polka-dot fabric for outer border and binding
- ¼ yard of red large-scale polka-dot fabric for inner border
- Large scrap *each* of 11 assorted fabrics for cats
- Small scraps of assorted fabrics for bow ties, collars, eyes, and noses
- 2¾ yards of backing fabric
- 45" x 55" piece of batting
- Embroidery floss in black, brown, and gray

Cutting

All measurements include ¼"-wide seam allowances.

From the light green fabric, cut:

- 8 strips, 2" x 42"; crosscut into:
  - 11 rectangles, 2" x 5"
  - 33 rectangles, 2" x 3½"
  - 55 squares, 2" x 2"
- 1 strip, 2⅜" x 42"; crosscut into 11 squares, 2⅜" x 2⅜". Cut each square once diagonally to yield 22 half-square triangles.

From *each* of the 11 assorted cat fabrics, cut:

- 1 square, 5" x 5" (11 squares total)
- 2 squares, 2⅜" x 2⅜" (22 squares total); cut each square once diagonally to yield 44 half-square triangles
- 1 square, 2" x 2" (11 squares total)

From the small scraps of assorted fabrics, cut:

- 11 bow-tie squares, 2⅜" x 2⅜"; cut each square once diagonally to yield 22 half-square triangles
- 11 collar squares, 2" x 2"

Over the years, my oldest daughter has rescued numerous cats from animal shelters. She encourages her family and friends to adopt cats and has a real talent for picking the perfect owner for each cat. Here are 11 good-looking fellows just waiting for a home—and in your quilt each one can be the lucky cat selected.

From the medium green checked fabric, cut:

- 5 squares, 11⅞" x 11⅞"; cut each square twice diagonally to yield 20 quarter-square triangles. (You will use 18.)
- 1 square, 11⅜" x 11⅜"; cut once diagonally to yield 2 half-square triangles
- 1 strip, 6⅛" x 42"; crosscut into 4 squares, 6⅛" x 6⅛". Cut each square once diagonally to yield 8 half-square triangles.
- 5 strips, 2½" x 42"

From the red large-scale polka-dot fabric, cut:

- 5 strips, 1" x 42"

From the red small-scale polka-dot fabric, cut:

- 10 strips, 2" x 42"

Making the Cat Blocks

1. To make one Cat block, draw a diagonal line from corner to corner on the wrong side of three of the 2" light green squares and one of the collar squares. Place each square on a corner of one 5" cat square, right sides together as shown. Sew on the marked lines,

trim to a ¼" seam allowance, and press the seams toward the triangle corners.

 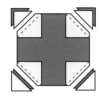

2. Sew two matching cat half-square triangles to two light green half-square triangles. Press the seam toward the cat fabric.

Make 2.

3. Sew two matching cat half-square triangles to two bow-tie half-square triangles. Press the seams toward the bow-tie fabric.

Make 2.

4. Sew a 2" x 3½" light green rectangle to a triangle square from step 3 as shown. Press the seam toward the rectangle.

Make 1.

5. Sew a triangle square from step 2 between two 2" light green squares. Press the seams toward the light green squares.

Make 1.

6. Sew the two strips from steps 4 and 5 to the sides of the unit from step 1 as shown. Press the seams toward the strips.

   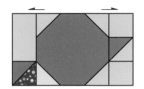

7. Sew a triangle square from step 2 between two 2" x 3½" light green rectangles. Press the seams toward the green rectangles.

Make 1.

8. Sew a triangle square from step 3 between the matching 2" cat-fabric square and a 2" x 5" light green rectangle as shown. Press the seams toward the cat-fabric square and rectangle.

Make 1.

9. Sew the two strips from steps 7 and 8 to the remaining sides of the unit as shown. Press the seams toward the strips.

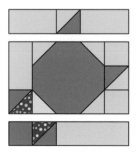 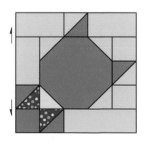

10. Repeat steps 1–9 to make a total of 11 different Cat blocks.

Appliquéing and Embroidering the Cat Eyes and Noses

1. Trace the pattern shapes on page 47, referring to the directions for needle-turn appliqué or fusible appliqué on pages 86–87. Cut the eyes and noses from the assorted small scraps.

2. Use the placement guide on page 47 to properly place each cat's eyes and nose. Baste or pin in place and appliqué.

3. Use two strands of embroidery floss to satin stitch the eyeballs. Outline the eyes and add the whiskers using stem stitch with two strands of embroidery floss.

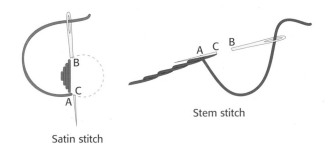

Satin stitch

Stem stitch

Assembling the Quilt

1. Arrange the Cat blocks into three vertical rows, with three Cat blocks in the middle row and four Cat blocks in the outside rows. Referring to the block layout, sew 18 green

checked quarter-square triangles to the sides of the Cat blocks. Press the seams towards the triangles. On the outside rows, sew the eight 6⅛" green checked half-square triangles to the top and bottom of the rows. Press the seams toward the triangles. On the middle row, sew the two 11⅜" green checked half-square triangles to the top and bottom of the row. Press the seams toward the triangles.

2. Sew all the diagonal seams to complete each row. Press the seams as shown. Sew the three rows together. Press the seams in one direction.

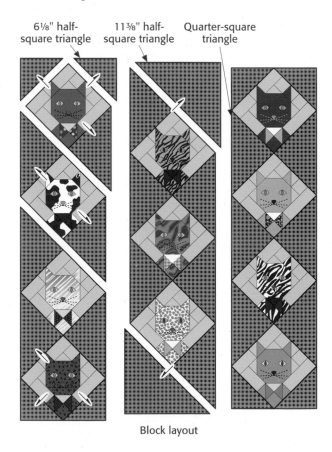

6⅛" half-square triangle 11⅜" half-square triangle Quarter-square triangle

Block layout

Adding the Borders

1. Sew the red large-scale polka-dot inner-border strips together end to end. Cut to make two strips that are 45" long and two that are 55" long. Repeat with the medium green checked middle-border strips and five of the red small-scale polka-dot outer-border strips.

2. Sew the border strips together in sets of three strips of the same length (green checked in the middle) and press all the seams toward the outer-border strips.

3. Referring to "Mitered Borders" on page 91, sew the borders to the quilt top.

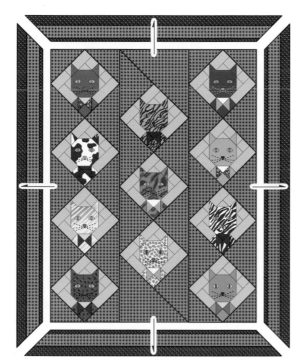

Quilt diagram

Finishing Your Quilt

Refer to "General Directions" on page 86 for specific directions regarding each of the following steps.

1. Layer the quilt top with batting and backing; baste.

2. Hand or machine quilt as desired. My suggestions include stipple quilting around each cat and making petal-type loops in the green checked background. Continuous-line quilted circles were added in the green checked border and a zigzag design was quilted in the outer red border.

3. Trim the batting and backing even with the quilt-top edges.

4. Referring to "Straight-Cut Binding" on page 94, prepare the remaining five red small-scale polka-dot strips for binding and sew the binding to the quilt.

Mr. Lucky appliqué patterns, and appliqué and embroidery placement guides

Add a ¼" seam allowance for finished-edge appliqué. Do not add a seam allowance for fusible appliqué.

Satin stitch
····· Stem stitch

Mr. Lucky Pillow

Finished pillow size: 16" x 16"

Materials

Yardages are based on 42"-wide fabrics.

- ⅝ yard of red small-scale polka-dot fabric for outside border and pillow back
- ⅜ yard of medium green checked fabric for setting triangles and border
- ⅛ yard of light green fabric for cat background
- ⅛ yard of red-and-black polka-dot fabric for inner border
- 18" x 18" piece of muslin for pillow-top backing
- Large scrap of fabric for cat
- Small scraps of fabric for bow tie, collar, eyes, and nose
- 18" x 18" piece of batting
- 16" pillow form
- Black embroidery floss

Cutting

All measurements include ¼"-wide seam allowances.

From the light green fabric, cut:
- 1 square, 2⅜" x 2⅜"; cut once diagonally to yield 2 half-square triangles
- 1 rectangle, 2" x 5"
- 3 rectangles, 2" x 3½"
- 5 squares, 2" x 2"

From the small scraps of fabric, cut:
- 1 bow-tie square, 2⅜" x 2⅜"; cut once diagonally to yield 2 half-square triangles
- 1 collar square, 2" x 2"

From the cat fabric, cut:
- 1 square, 5" x 5"
- 2 squares, 2⅜" x 2⅜"; cut each square once diagonally to yield 4 half-square triangles
- 1 square, 2" x 2"

From the medium green checked fabric, cut:
- 2 squares, 6⅛" x 6⅛"; cut each square once diagonally to yield 4 half-square triangles
- 2 strips, 2" x 42"; crosscut into:
  - 2 strips, 2" x 12"
  - 2 strips, 2" x 15"

From the red-and-black polka-dot fabric, cut:
- 2 strips, 1" x 42"; crosscut into:
  - 2 strips, 1" x 11"
  - 2 strips, 1" x 12"

From the red small-scale polka-dot fabric, cut:
- 2 rectangles, 13" x 17"
- 2 strips, 1½" x 42"; crosscut into:
  - 2 strips, 1½" x 15"
  - 2 strips, 1½" x 17"

Making the Pillow Top

1. To make one block for the pillow center, follow steps 1–9 of "Making the Cat Blocks" on page 45 and steps 1–3 of "Appliquéing and Embroidering the Cat Eyes and Noses" on page 46.

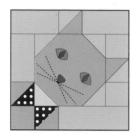

2. Sew medium green checked triangles to opposite sides of the center block. Then sew two more triangles to the two remaining sides. Press all the seams toward the triangles.

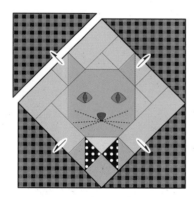

3. Sew the 11" red-and-black polka-dot strips to the top and bottom of the block, and then sew the 12" strips to each side. Press all the seams toward the border strips.

4. Sew the 12" medium green checked strips to the top and bottom of the block, and then sew the 15" strips to each side. Press all the seams toward the medium green checked border strips.

5. Sew the 15" red small-scale polka-dot strips to the top and bottom of the block, and then sew the 17" strips to each side. Press all the seams toward the red small-scale polka-dot border strips.

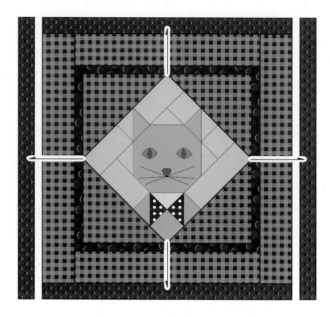

Quilting the Pillow Top

Refer to "Quilting" on page 92 for specific directions regarding each of the following steps.

1. Layer the muslin, batting, and pillow top. Baste using thread, pins, or basting spray to hold the layers together.

2. Machine or hand quilt. This pillow was simply quilted in the ditch.

3. Trim the excess batting and muslin so the pillow top measures 17" x 17".

Assembling the Pillow

1. On each 13" x 17" backing rectangle, turn under ¼" on one of the 17" edges and press. Turn under again by 1"; press and edgestitch close to the inner fold.

2. Place the backing rectangles right sides together with the pillow top, overlapping the stitched edges of the backing rectangles and keeping the raw edges even. Pin all sides, and then sew completely around the pillow with a ½" seam. Clip the corners at an angle to reduce bulk, being careful to leave at least ¼" from each stitched corner.

Overlap.

3. Turn the completed pillow cover right side out and press. Insert the pillow form.

Pocket Quilt

Finished quilt size: 39½" x 47½"

Materials

Yardages are based on 42"-wide fabrics.

- 7/8 yard of red large-scale polka-dot fabric for borders and binding
- 5/8 yard of multicolored print for pockets
- 1/2 yard of light blue fabric for sky
- 1/4 yard of blue polka-dot fabric for Stripe block
- 1/4 yard of black-and-white checked fabric for Stripe block
- 1/4 yard of green print for Sun block
- 1/4 yard of yellow print for Sun block
- 1/4 yard of green polka-dot fabric for Tree block
- 1/8 yard of red-and-black polka-dot fabric for Stripe block
- 1/8 yard of yellow-and-white checked fabric for House block
- Scraps of assorted fabrics for houses, roofs, doors, windows, chimneys, tree trunks, sun, strips for Tree blocks and Pocket blocks, and Velcro appliquéd circles
- 2 3/4 yards of backing fabric
- 45" x 52" piece of batting
- 1/2 yard of lightweight fusible web
- Black thread
- 4 Velcro hook-and-loop circle fasteners, 3/4" diameter

Cutting

All measurements include 1/4"-wide seam allowances.

From the multicolored print, cut:
- 2 strips, 5 1/2" x 42"; crosscut into:
  - 4 rectangles, 5 1/2" x 9 1/2"
  - 4 squares, 5 1/2" x 5 1/2"
- 1 strip, 4 1/2" x 42"; crosscut into 4 squares, 4 1/2" x 4 1/2". Cut each square once diagonally to yield 8 half-square triangles.

From the yellow print, cut:
- 1 strip, 3 1/2" x 42"; crosscut into 4 rectangles, 3 1/2" x 5 1/2"

From the light blue fabric, cut:
- 1 strip, 5 1/2" x 42"; crosscut into:
  - 4 squares, 5 1/2" x 5 1/2"
  - 4 rectangles, 1 1/2" x 5 1/2"
- 1 strip, 3 1/2" x 42"; crosscut into 8 squares, 3 1/2" x 3 1/2"
- 1 strip, 3 3/8" x 42"; crosscut into 8 squares, 3 3/8" x 3 3/8"
- 1 strip, 2 1/2" x 42"; crosscut into 8 pieces, 2 1/2" x 2 3/4"

From the green print, cut:
- 1 strip, 3 1/2" x 42"; crosscut into 4 strips, 3 1/2" x 8 1/2"

From the yellow-and-white checked fabric, cut:
- 1 strip, 2 1/2" x 42"; crosscut into 4 strips, 2 1/2" x 8 1/2"

From the green polka-dot fabric, cut:
- 2 squares, 6 1/4" x 6 1/4"

From the red-and-black polka-dot fabric, cut:
- 1 strip, 2 1/2" x 42"

From the blue polka-dot fabric, cut:
- 1 strip, 3 1/2" x 42"

From the black-and-white checked fabric, cut:
- 1 strip, 3 1/2" x 42"

From the red large-scale polka-dot fabric, cut:
- 4 strips, 4" x 42"; crosscut into:
  - 2 strips, 4" x 40½"
  - 2 strips, 4" x 39½"
- 5 strips, 2" x 42"

Making the Pocket Block

1. To make one Pocket block, sew two of the multicolored half-square triangles right sides together, stitching on the short sides. Trim the corner tip; turn right side out and press. Sew a Velcro loop fastener to the pocket flap ⅞" from the tip. For a more finished look, turn the flap over and hand appliqué a circle over the stitching using the circle pattern on page 58 and one of the assorted scraps.

Raw edges

Trim.

⅞"

2. Fold a multicolored rectangle in half cross-wise, wrong sides together. Sew a Velcro hook fastener in the center, ½" down from the folded end. Place the folded rectangle on top of a 5½" multicolored square as shown and machine baste a scant ¼" seam around the sides and bottom.

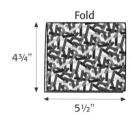

Fold

4¾"

5½"

½"

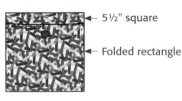

5½" square

Folded rectangle

Baste a scant
¼" seam.

3. From one of the assorted scraps, cut two strips, 2" x 5½", and two strips, 2" x 8½". Sew the 5½" strips to each side of the unit from step 2. Press the seams toward the strips.

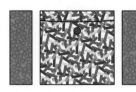

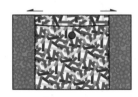

4. Place the pocket flap from step 1 in the center of the pocket unit from step 3 and baste in place using a scant ¼" seam. Sew the 8½" strips from step 3 to the top and bottom of the pocket. Press the seams toward the strips.

Baste a scant
¼" seam.

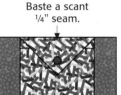

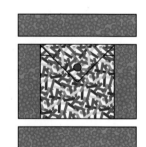

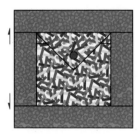

5. Repeat steps 1–4 to make three more Pocket blocks.

Making the Sun Block

The Sun block has appliqué shapes that were fused and machine appliquéd. Refer to "Fusible Appliqué" on page 87 for detailed instructions.

1. To make one Sun block, sew a yellow print rectangle to the bottom of a 5½" light blue square. Press the seam toward the yellow rectangle. Sew a green print strip to the right side of the block. Press the seam toward the green strip.

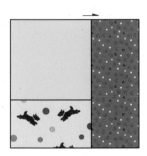

2. Trace the sun patterns on page 58. Cut the center circle and rays for the sun from the assorted scraps. Place the prepared shapes in the middle of the light blue square and fuse.

3. Machine appliqué the edges of the pieces using matching thread color.

4. Repeat steps 1–3 to make three more Sun blocks.

Making the House Block

The House block has appliqué shapes that were fused and machine appliquéd. Refer to "Fusible Appliqué" on page 87 for detailed instructions.

1. To make one House block, cut a 3½" x 6½" rectangle for the roof and a 5½" x 6½" rectangle for the house from the assorted scraps.

2. Sew the roof rectangle to the house rectangle as shown. Press the seam toward the roof. Draw a diagonal line corner to corner on the wrong side of two 3½" light blue squares. Place one square on each of the roof corners as shown and sew on the marked line. Trim to a ¼" seam allowance and press the seams toward the triangles.

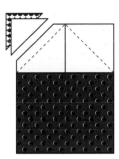

3. Sew a yellow-and-white checked strip to the right side of the House block. Press the seam toward the strip.

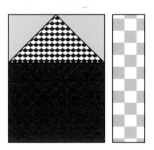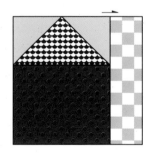

4. Trace the pattern shapes from page 58 for the door, window, and chimney. Cut one door, three windows, and one chimney from the assorted scraps. Place the prepared shapes on the House block as shown on page 56 and fuse.

5. Machine appliqué the edges of the pieces using matching thread. Use black thread and a zigzag stitch to make the windowpanes.

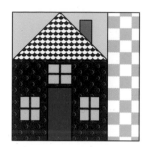

6. Repeat steps 1–5 to make three more House blocks.

Making the Tree Blocks

1. Following the directions on page 89 for "Quick and Easy Flying Geese," use the two green polka-dot squares and the eight 3⅜" light blue squares to make eight flying-geese units, 3" x 5½" unfinished.

2. Sew two units together along the length of the rectangles as shown to make four pairs. Press the seam toward the bottom unit.

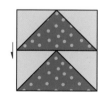

Make 4.

3. From a brown fabric scrap, cut four strips, 1" x 2½". Sew each strip between two 2½" x 2¾" light blue pieces as shown. Press the seams toward the brown strip.

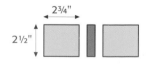

Make 4.

4. Sew the trunk unit from step 3 to the tree unit from step 2 as shown. Press the seam toward the trunk unit. Sew a 1½" x 5½" light blue rectangle to the top of each Tree block. Press the seam toward the sky strip.

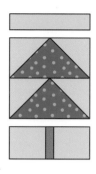

Make 4.

5. From one of the assorted scraps, cut four strips, 2" x 8½". From a different scrap cut four strips, 2" x 8½". Sew one of each strip to each side of the Tree blocks. Press the seams toward the strips.

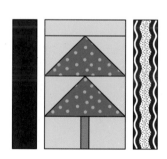
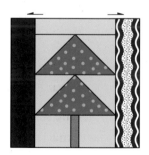

Make 4.

Making the Stripe Blocks

Sew the red-and-black polka-dot strip between the blue polka-dot strip and the black-and-white checked strip. Press the seams in one direction. Cut the strip into four blocks, 8½" wide.

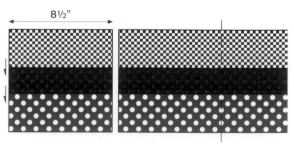

Cut 4 blocks.

Assembling the Quilt

1. Referring to the block layout below, arrange the blocks in five rows of four blocks each.

2. Sew the blocks together into rows; press the seams in opposite directions from row to row. Sew the rows together and press.

Block layout

Adding the Borders

1. Sew the 40½" red large-scale polka-dot strips to the sides of the quilt top. Press the seams toward the strips.

2. Sew the 39½" red large-scale polka-dot strips to the top and bottom of the quilt top. Press the seams toward the strips.

Quilt diagram

Finishing Your Quilt

Refer to "General Directions" on page 86 for specific directions regarding each of the following steps.

1. Layer the quilt top with batting and backing; baste.

2. Hand or machine quilt as desired. My suggestions include quilting in the ditch and around the appliqué shapes. Edgestitch around the pockets to make them secure.

3. Trim the batting and backing even with the quilt-top edges.

4. Referring to "Straight-Cut Binding" on page 94, prepare the 2"-wide red large-scale polka-dot strips for binding and sew the binding to the quilt.

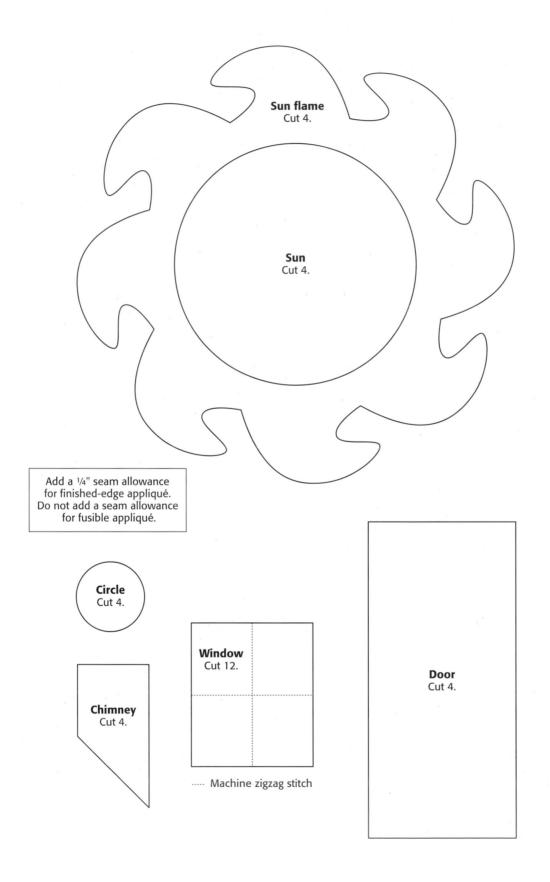

Sun flame
Cut 4.

Sun
Cut 4.

Add a ¼" seam allowance
for finished-edge appliqué.
Do not add a seam allowance
for fusible appliqué.

Circle
Cut 4.

Window
Cut 12.

Chimney
Cut 4.

Door
Cut 4.

····· Machine zigzag stitch

Spotty Dog

Finished quilt size: 41½" x 57½"

Materials

Yardages are based on 42"-wide fabrics.

- 1⅜ yards *total* of 8 to 10 different light plaid or striped fabrics for blocks
- 1⅛ yards of medium blue plaid fabric for outer border and binding
- ¾ yard *total* of 12 different medium plaid or striped fabrics for blocks and bows
- ⅝ yard *total* of 6 different dark plaid or solid fabrics for blocks
- ⅜ yard of dark blue fabric for inner border
- ¼ yard of black-and-white polka-dot fabric for Spotty
- 2¾ yards of backing fabric
- 45" x 62" piece of batting

Cutting

All measurements include ¼"-wide seam allowances.

From the light plaid or striped fabrics, cut:
- 12 squares, 6⅞" x 6⅞"; cut each square once diagonally to yield 24 half-square triangles
- 72 squares, 2⅞" x 2⅞", cut each square once diagonally to yield 144 half-square triangles
- 24 squares, 2½" x 2½"

From the medium plaid or striped fabrics, cut:
- 12 squares, 6⅞" x 6⅞"; cut each square once diagonally to yield 24 half-square triangles

From the dark plaid or solid fabrics, cut:
- 72 squares, 2⅞" x 2⅞", cut each square once diagonally to yield 144 half-square triangles

From the dark blue fabric, cut:
- 6 strips, 1½" x 42"

From the medium blue plaid fabric, cut:
- 6 strips, 4" x 42"
- 6 strips, 2" x 42"

Everyone loves a Scottie dog, especially children. To make "Spotty Dog" in this classic style, pull out your plaid collection and make it scrappy. For a different look, make it from small colorful prints.

Making the Blocks

1. With right sides together, sew the 6⅞" light plaid or striped half-square triangles to the medium plaid or striped half-square triangles to make 24 triangle squares. Press the seams toward the darker fabric.

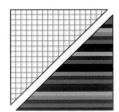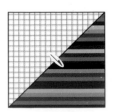

Make 24.

2. Sew the 2⅞" light plaid or striped half-square triangles to the dark plaid or striped half-square triangles to make 144 triangle squares. Mix and match the colors as desired. Press the seams toward the darker fabric.

Make 144.

3. Sew the triangle squares from step 2 into sets of three. Make sure that half of the units face one way and the other half face the other way as shown; press.

Make 24.   Make 24.

4. Using the large triangle squares from step 1, the 2½" light plaid squares, and the triangle strips from step 3, lay out the pieces as shown. Sew the pieces together into rows. Press the seams away from the triangle strips. Sew the two rows together and press.

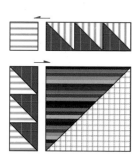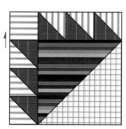

Make 24.

5. Sew the units from step 4 into pairs and press the seams to the right. Sew the paired blocks together as shown. Press the seams in one direction.

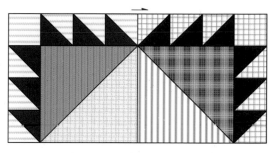

Make 12.

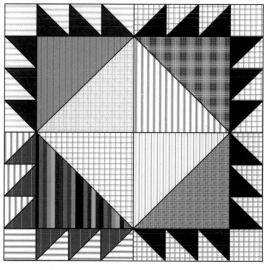

Make 6.

Appliquéing the Dogs

The dogs were appliquéd using the freezer-paper method. You can use your favorite technique. Refer to "Appliquéing" on page 86 for detailed instructions.

1. Trace the pattern shapes for the dog and bow on page 63, remembering to reverse three of the dogs and three of the bows. Cut the dogs from the black-and-white polka-dot and the bows from the medium plaid scraps.

2. Center the prepared appliqué shapes on the middle of the pieced blocks. Baste or pin in place. Appliqué the dog first and then add the bow.

Assembling the Quilt

1. Referring to the block layout, arrange the blocks in three rows of two blocks each. The dogs face each other in the top and bottom rows and face away from each other in the middle row.

2. Sew the blocks together into rows; press the seams in opposite directions from row to row. Sew the rows together and press.

Block layout

Adding the Borders

1. Sew the dark blue strips together end to end. Cut to make two strips that are 45" and two that are 62". Repeat with the 4"-wide medium blue plaid strips.

2. Sew each inner-border strip to the outer-border strip of the same length. Press the seams toward the outer-border strips.

3. Referring to "Mitered Borders" on page 91, sew the borders to the quilt top.

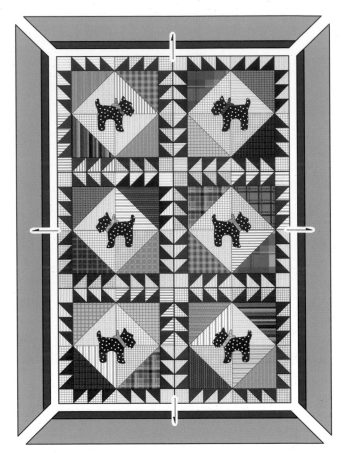

Quilt diagram

Finishing Your Quilt

Refer to "General Directions" on page 86 for specific directions regarding each of the following steps.

1. Layer the quilt top with batting and backing, baste.

2. Hand or machine quilt as desired. My suggestions include quilting in the ditch and around the appliqués.

3. Trim the batting and backing even with the quilt-top edges.

4. Referring to "Straight-Cut Binding" on page 94, prepare the 2"-wide medium blue plaid binding strips and sew the binding to the quilt.

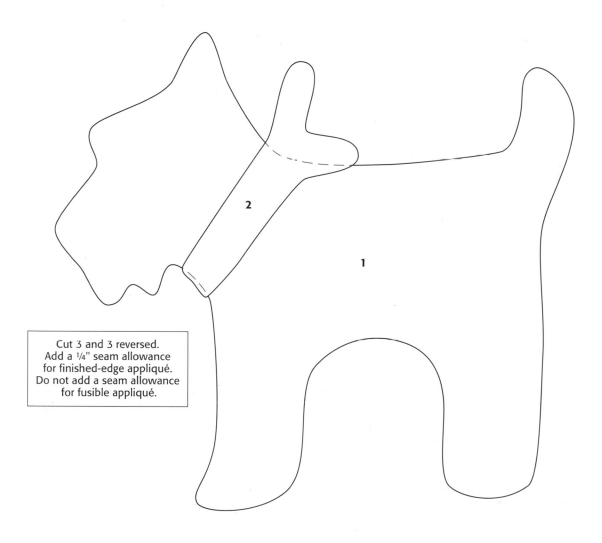

Cut 3 and 3 reversed.
Add a ¼" seam allowance
for finished-edge appliqué.
Do not add a seam allowance
for fusible appliqué.

Small Pillow

Finished pillow size: 16" x 12"

Materials

Yardage is based on 42"-wide fabric.

- ¾ yard of pillow ticking fabric for pillow cover
- 2 yards of ⅜" cording
- 12" x 16" pillow form

Cutting

All measurements include ¼"-wide seam allowances.

From the ticking fabric, cut:

- 3 bias strips, 1" x 23" (Refer to "Bias-Cut Binding" on page 95 for directions on cutting the strips.)
- 2 rectangles, 12½" x 16½"

Making the Cording

1. Join the bias strips as shown.

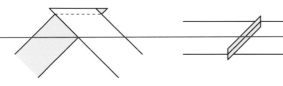

2. Center the cording on the wrong side of the bias strip and wrap the fabric around it with the raw edges even.

3. Using the zipper foot, machine baste along the cord to enclose it in the fabric strip. Leave the first 2" unsewn.

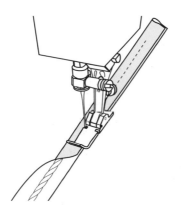

Sometimes kids have special little pillows that they love and carry about for comfort. When I make a kid's pillow, I use a heavy fabric for the cover so the pillow can be tossed into the washer and machine dried over and over. There is nothing better than a clean, warm pillow fresh out of the dryer for naptime!

Making the Pillow Cover

1. Round off all four corners of the two 12½" x 16½" rectangles to make it easier to apply the cording.

Round off the corners.

2. Place the covered cording on the right side of one of the rectangles. Start stitching in the middle of one side. Using the zipper foot, baste the cording in place. Begin stitching about 2" from one end of the covered cording. Stitch right on the cording seam line around the rectangle, stopping 1" from the beginning of the cording.

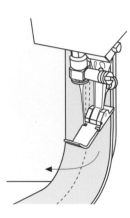

3. Cut away the excess cording, leaving 1" extra. Trim the cord inside so that it butts against the beginning piece. Turn under ½" at the trimmed end of the covered cording and slip the other end inside as shown. Complete the stitching.

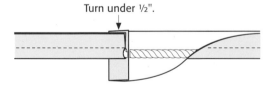

To join the cording, trim the cord so the ends meet.

Overlap to cover the ends of the cord. Stitch.

4. Place the two rectangles right sides together and pin. Sew on the side where you can see the cording seam. Stitch just a needle's width to the left of the seam. Leave a 10" opening on one side.

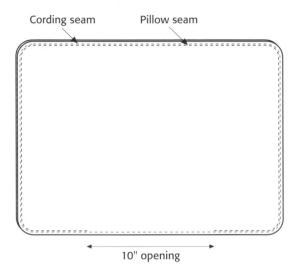

5. Turn the pillow cover right side out and insert the pillow form. Slip-stitch the opening closed.

Little Dog Pillowcase

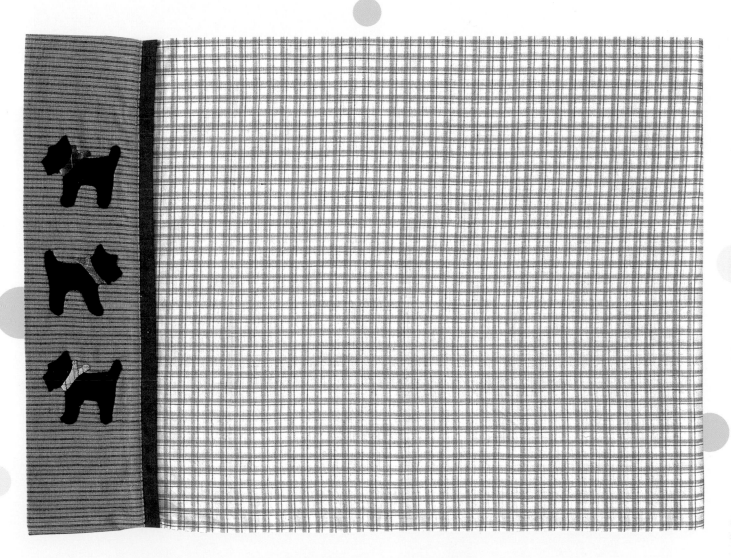

Finished pillowcase size: 18" x 13½"

Materials

Yardages are based on 42"-wide fabrics.

- ⅝ yard of plaid fabric for pillowcase panel
- ⅜ yard of fabric for contrasting band
- ⅛ yard of fabric for accent strip
- Scraps of black and plaid fabrics for appliqué

Cutting

All measurements include ¼"-wide seam allowances.

From the contrasting-band fabric, cut:

- 1 strip, 7" x 28"

From the accent strip fabric, cut:

- 1 strip, 1" x 28"

From the plaid fabric, cut:

- 1 rectangle, 16" x 28"

Appliquéing the Dogs

The dogs were appliquéd using the needle-turn method. You can use your favorite technique. Refer to "Appliquéing" on page 86 for detailed instructions.

1. Trace the pattern shapes for the dog and bow on page 69. Remember to reverse one dog and one bow. Cut the dogs from the black scraps and the bows from the plaid scraps.

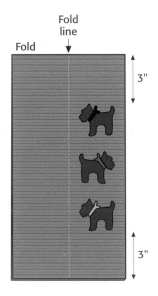

Pillowcases are my favorite projects because they're fast and easy to make. I usually make them to match the quilt I've just finished. It is a good way to use the leftover fabrics. And they make the perfect gift for the new big brother or sister.

2. Fold the contrasting band in half lengthwise, wrong sides together, and press. Now fold the band in half crosswise so you have a reference for where to place your appliqués. Unfold the band and place the three prepared appliqué dogs on it as shown. Baste or pin in place. Appliqué the dogs first and then add the bows.

Making the Pillowcase

1. Fold the accent strip in half lengthwise with wrong sides together and raw edges even; press.

2. Place the folded accent strip along the long edge closest to the appliqué. Machine baste a scant ¼" from the raw edges.

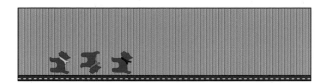

3. With right sides together, pin the accent edge of the band to one edge of the pillowcase panel. Sew ¼" from the raw edge. Press the seam toward the band.

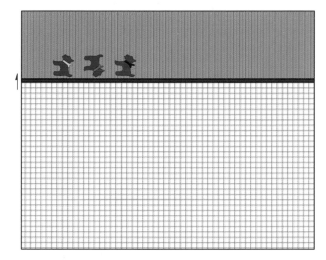

4. Turn the raw edge of the contrasting band under ¼". Fold the pillowcase in half lengthwise with right sides together. Sew ¼" from the raw edge, sewing along the bottom and around the side of the pillowcase.

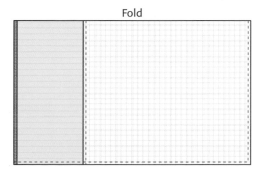

Turn under ¼". Sew the raw edges together.

5. Turn the band to the inside of the pillowcase with the folded edge just past the stitching line; press. Machine baste in place all the way around the pillowcase.

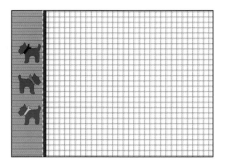

Baste.

6. Turn the pillowcase right side out. Edgestitch along the band seam all the way around the pillowcase. Remove the basting.

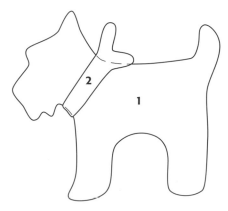

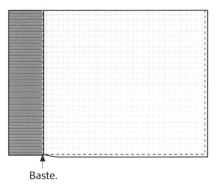

Cut 2 and 1 reversed.
Add a ¼" seam allowance
for finished-edge appliqué.
Do not add a seam allowance
for fusible appliqué.

Boxed Dots

Finished quilt size: 54½" x 63½". Quilted by Nona King.

Materials

Yardages are based on 42"-wide fabrics.

- 1⅛ yards of small-scale black-on-red polka-dot fabric for outer border and binding
- ⅞ yard of black-on-green polka-dot fabric for blocks
- ½ yard of large-scale black-on-red polka-dot fabric for blocks
- ½ yard of blue-on-white polka-dot fabric for blocks
- ½ yard of purple polka-dot fabric for blocks
- ½ yard of yellow-on-black polka-dot fabric for blocks
- ⅜ yard of yellow-on-orange polka-dot fabric for blocks
- ⅜ yard of blue polka-dot fabric for blocks
- ⅜ yard of black fabric for inner border
- 3½ yards of fabric for backing
- 60" x 69" piece of batting

Cutting

All measurements include ¼"-wide seam allowances.

From the blue-on-white polka-dot fabric, cut:
- 7 strips, 2" x 42"; crosscut into 70 rectangles, 2" x 3½"

From the large-scale black-on-red polka-dot fabric, cut:
- 4 strips, 3½" x 42"; crosscut into 35 squares, 3½" x 3½"

From the black-on-green polka-dot fabric, cut:
- 12 strips, 2" x 14"; crosscut into 70 rectangles, 2" x 6½"

From the purple polka-dot fabric, cut:
- 7 strips, 2" x 42"; crosscut into 70 rectangles, 2" x 3½"

This quilt is a little larger than the others in this book, and that makes it just the right size for the move from the crib to a youth bed. It's made using one easy block, so it goes together quickly. Play with colors and polka-dot fabrics to make this one fantastically fun!

From the yellow-on-black polka-dot fabric, cut:
- 7 strips, 2" x 42"; crosscut into 70 rectangles, 2" x 3½"

From the yellow-on-orange polka-dot fabric, cut:
- 5 strips, 2" x 42"; crosscut into 40 rectangles, 2" x 5"

From the blue polka-dot fabric, cut:
- 5 strips, 2" x 42"; crosscut into 40 rectangles, 2" x 5"

From the black fabric, cut:
- 6 strips, 1½" x 42"

From the small-scale black-on-red polka-dot fabric, cut:
- 6 strips, 4" x 42"
- 6 strips, 2" x 42"

Making the Blocks

This quilt is made from one block, but in every other row the block is missing a set of strips. You will be making 20 blocks, 9" x 9" (finished), and 15 blocks, 9" x 6" (finished).

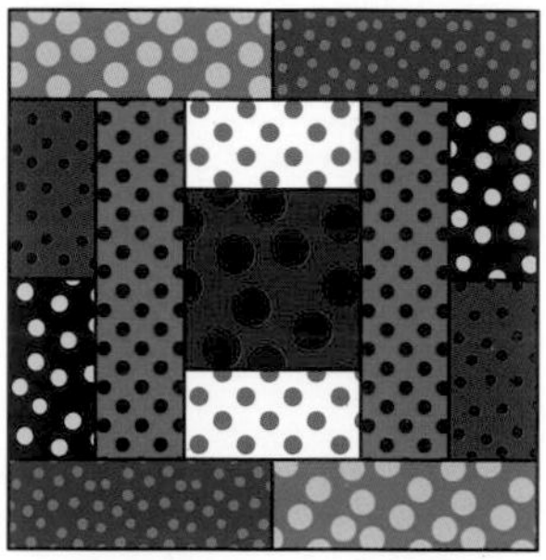

9" x 9" finished block

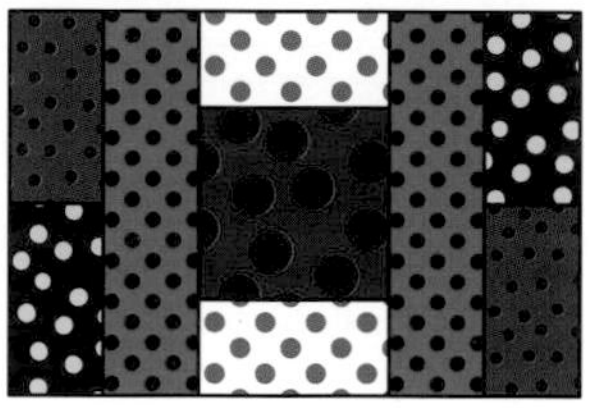

9" x 6" finished block

1. Sew two blue-on-white rectangles to the top and bottom of a large-scale black-on-red polka-dot square. Press the seams toward the strips.

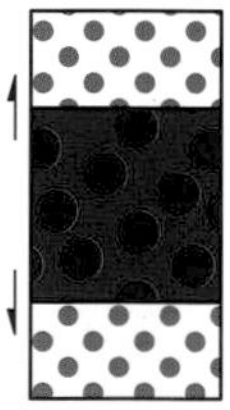

Make 35.

2. Sew a black-on-green rectangle to each side of a unit from step 1. Press the seams toward the black-on-green rectangles.

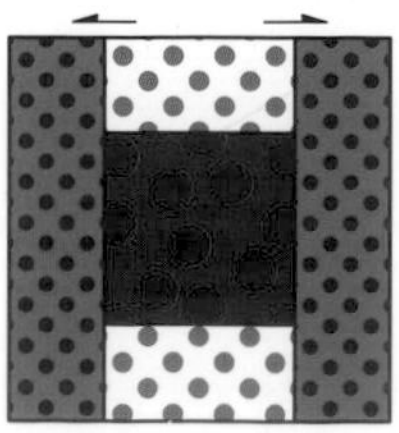

Make 35.

3. Sew a purple polka-dot rectangle to one end of each yellow-on-black rectangle. Press the seams toward the yellow-on-black rectangles.

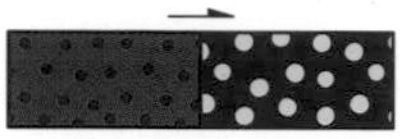

Make 70.

4. Sew the strips from step 3 to the sides of the units from step 2. Place the yellow-on-black rectangles on the bottom-left side and on the top-right side as shown. Press the seams toward the strips.

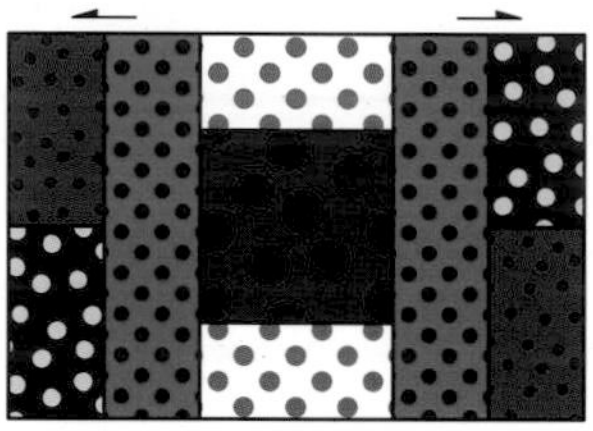

Make 35.

5. Sew each yellow-on-orange rectangle to one end of a blue polka-dot rectangle. Press the seams toward the blue rectangles.

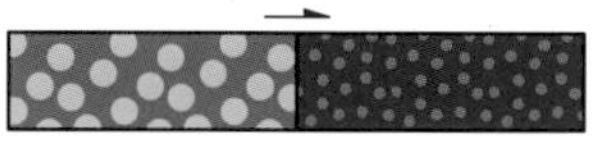

Make 40.

6. Sew the strips from step 5 to the top and bottom of 20 of the units from step 4. Place the yellow-on-orange rectangles on the top-left side and on the bottom-right side as shown. Press the seams toward the strips.

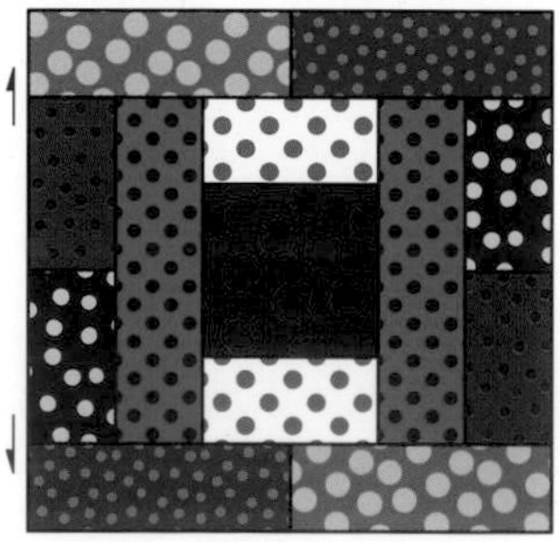

Make 20.

Assembling the Quilt

1. Referring to the block layout below, arrange the blocks in seven rows of five blocks each as shown. Start the first row with the full block and alternate every other row with the shorter block, ending with a full-block row.

2. Sew the blocks together into rows and press the seams in opposite directions from row the row. Sew the rows together; press.

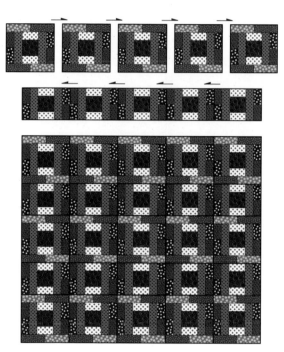

Block layout

Adding the Borders

Referring to "Straight-Cut Borders" on page 90, add the 1½"-wide black strips for the inner border and the 4"-wide small-scale black-on-red polka-dot strips for the outer border.

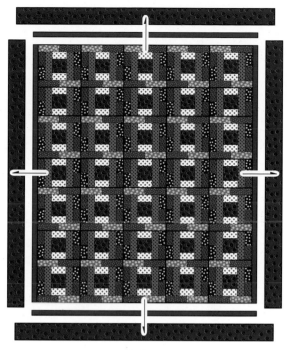

Quilt diagram

Finishing Your Quilt

Refer to "General Directions" on page 86 for specific directions regarding each of the following steps.

1. Layer the quilt top with the batting and backing; baste.

2. Machine or hand quilt as desired. My suggestions include quilting in a random free-motion pattern in the blocks and border and straight stitching around the inner border.

3. Trim the batting and backing even with the quilt-top edges.

4. Referring to "Straight-Cut Binding" on page 94, prepare the 2"-wide small-scale black-on-red polka-dot strips for binding and sew the binding to the quilt.

Little Dottie

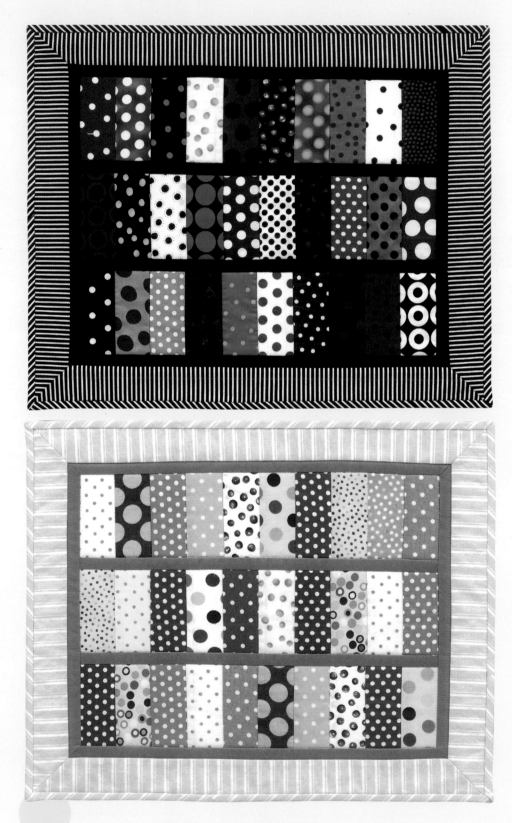

Finished quilt size: 15½" x 19"

Materials

Yardages are based on 42"-wide fabrics.

- ⅝ yard of striped fabric for borders and binding
- ¼ yard of solid for sashing strips and inner border
- Scraps of 30 different polka-dot fabrics for vertical rows
- 1 fat quarter for backing
- 18" x 22" piece of batting

Cutting

All measurements include ¼"-wide seam allowances.

From *each* of the polka-dot fabric scraps, cut:
- 1 rectangle, 2" x 4" (30 rectangles total)

From the solid, cut:
- 3 strips, 1" x 42"; crosscut into:
  - 2 strips, 1" x 15½"
  - 2 strips, 1" x 22"
  - 2 strips, 1" x 18"

From the striped fabric, cut:
- 2 strips, 2" x 42"; crosscut into:
  - 2 strips, 2" x 22"
  - 2 strips, 2" x 18"
- 4 bias-binding strips, 2" x approximately 20" (Refer to "Bias-Cut Binding" on page 95 for directions on cutting the strips.)

Making the Vertical Rows

1. Sew 10 polka-dot rectangles together along the length of each to make each vertical row. Press the seams in one direction.

Make 3 rows.

"Little Dottie" was so much fun that I had to make two! The first is bright and bold with a different polka-dot fabric in each strip. In the second, I repeated strips using a candy-colored palette. This project can be a sweet little doll quilt or a superfast gift for a friend's sewing room.

2. Sew the 15½" solid strips between the rows as shown. Press the seams toward the strips.

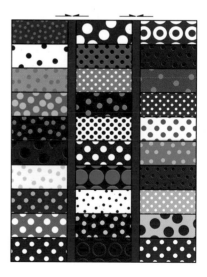

Adding the Borders

1. With right sides together and stitching along the length, sew each 1"-wide solid strip to a 2"-wide straight-cut striped strip of the same length. Press the seams toward the outer-border strips.

2. Referring to "Mitered Borders" on page 91, sew the borders to the quilt top.

Finishing Your Quilt

Refer to "General Directions" on page 86 for specific directions regarding each of the following steps.

1. Layer the quilt top with batting and backing; baste.

2. Machine or hand quilt as desired. My suggestions include stitching in the ditch around the rectangles and the outside sashing strips.

3. Trim the batting and backing even with the quilt-top edges.

4. Referring to "Bias-Cut Binding" on page 95, prepare the 2"-wide striped bias strips for binding and sew the binding to the quilt.

Designer Tip

For a different theme, try using stripes, plaids, or solids instead of polka dots. What could be easier?

Flannel Blocks with Polka Dots

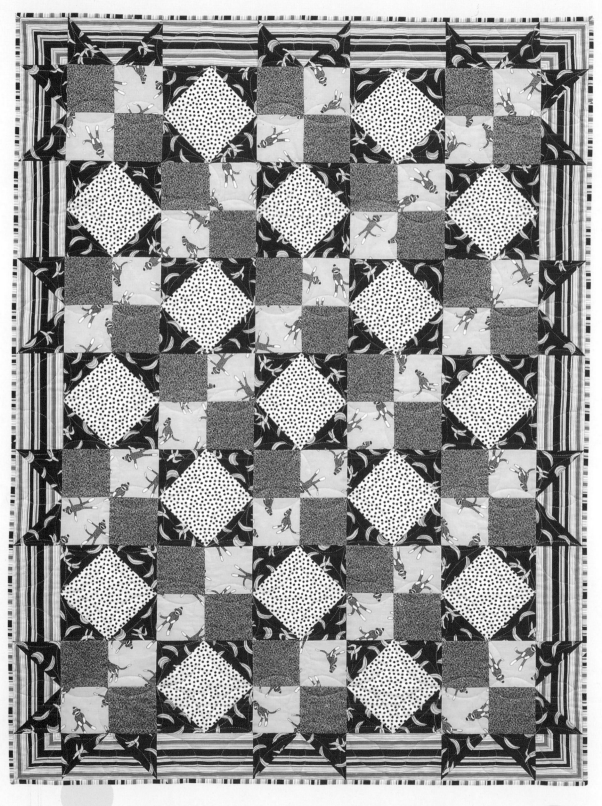

Finished quilt size: 42½" x 56½". Quilted by Nona King.

Materials

Yardages are based on 42"-wide fabrics.

- 1½ yards of striped flannel for borders and binding*
- 1⅛ yards of red print flannel for blocks and border
- ⅝ yard of polka-dot flannel for blocks
- ⅝ yard of brown print flannel for blocks
- ⅝ yard of yellow print flannel for blocks
- 3 yards of backing fabric
- 48" x 62" piece of batting

If you are not matching the stripes, you will need only 1⅛ yards.

Cutting

All measurements include ¼"-wide seam allowances.

From the red print flannel, cut:

- 5 strips, 4¼" x 42"; crosscut into 34 squares, 4½" x 4½". Cut each square once diagonally to yield 68 half-square triangles.
- 3 strips, 4" x 42"; crosscut into 28 squares, 4" x 4"

From the polka-dot flannel, cut:

- 3 strips, 5½" x 42"; crosscut into 17 squares, 5½" x 5½"

From the brown print flannel, cut:

- 4 strips, 4" x 42"

From the yellow print flannel, cut:

- 4 strips, 4" x 42"

For cozy, curl-up comfort, nothing is as inviting as a flannel quilt. With all the fantastic flannel fabrics on the market to choose from, you may want to make this project more than once. Try the striped border for the first one and a polka-dot border for the second!

From the striped flannel, cut:

- 3 strips, 7½" x 42"; crosscut into 24 rectangles, 4" x 7½"*
- 1 strip, 4⅜" x 42"; crosscut into 4 squares, 4⅜" x 4⅜"**
- 5 strips, 2" x 42"

Cut identical pieces, centering the same color stripe in each one.
**Cut 8 squares if the stripes are not symmetrical.*

Making the Polka-Dot Blocks

Sew red triangles to opposite sides of each polka-dot square. Press the seams toward the triangles. Add two more red triangles to the remaining edges in the same manner and press. Check the block measurements and trim to a 7½" square if necessary.

Make 17.

Making the Four Patch Blocks

1. Sew each brown strip to a yellow strip along the length of the strips. Press the seams toward the brown strips. Make four strip sets and cut them into 36 segments, 4" wide.

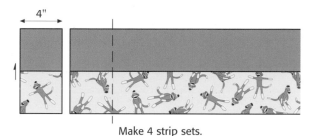

Make 4 strip sets.
Cut 36 segments.

2. Sew the segments into pairs as shown to make Four Patch blocks. Press the seams in one direction.

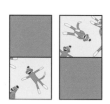 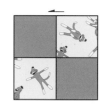

Make 18.

Making the Border

1. On the wrong side of each 4" red square, draw a diagonal line with a fabric marker or pencil. Place a marked square at the left end of a striped rectangle with the diagonal line positioned as shown. Stitch on the line, cut away the corner ¼" from the stitching, and press the seam toward the triangle. Repeat to add a red square to the other end of the rectangle as shown.

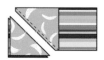

Make 14.

2. Stack two of the four striped squares with the stripes running vertically and two with the stripes running horizontally. Cut each stack of squares once diagonally as shown, for a total of 8 triangles. If the stripes are not symmetrical, you don't need to worry about the orientation; cut the eight 4⅜" striped squares once diagonally to make 16 triangles. Use 8 of these triangles to make four matching corners.

Cut 2 squares with strips oriented vertically.   Cut 2 squares with strips oriented horizontally.

3. Sew the vertical-striped triangles to the horizontal-striped triangles in pairs, taking care to match the stripes along the diagonal seam. Press the seam open.

Make 4.

4. Assemble the top and bottom border strips using the pieced squares, pieced striped rectangles, and striped rectangles in the order shown. Press the seams toward the pieced squares and striped rectangles.

Make 2.

Assembling the Quilt

1. Arrange the Four Patch blocks and the Polka-Dot blocks in rows. Make four rows that begin and end with a Four Patch block and add a pieced striped rectangle to each end as shown. Sew the blocks together and press the seams toward the Four Patch blocks.

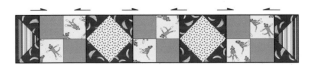

Make 4.

2. Make three rows that begin and end with a Polka-Dot block and add a plain striped rectangle to each end as shown. Sew the blocks together and press the seams toward the Four Patch blocks and plain striped rectangles.

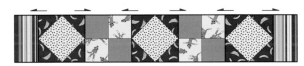

Make 3.

3. Sew the three rows from step 2 between the four rows from step 1. Press the seams in one direction. Sew the two border strips to the top and bottom of the quilt top and press as shown.

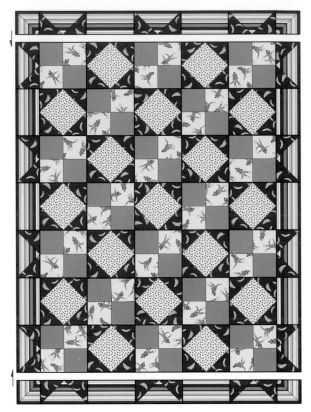

Quilt diagram

Finishing Your Quilt

Refer to "General Directions" on page 86 for specific directions regarding each of the following steps.

1. Layer the quilt top with batting and backing; baste.

2. Hand or machine quilt as desired. My suggestions include quilting an allover design of interwoven circles and loops.

3. Trim the batting and backing even with the quilt-top edges.

4. Referring to "Straight-Cut Binding" on page 94, prepare the 2"-wide striped strips for binding and sew the binding to the quilt.

Naptime Monkey

Finished quilt size: 21½" x 28½"

Materials

Yardages are based on 42"-wide fabrics.

- ⅛ yard *each* of 9 assorted prints for the quilt blocks *or* cut 42 squares, 3½" x 3½", from scrap fabrics
- ⅜ yard of striped fabric for pillow
- ¼ yard of polka-dot fabric for bottom sheet
- ⅛ yard of red print for top sheet
- Scraps of brown, cream, black, red, and polka-dot fabrics for the appliqué
- ¼ yard of red-and-white fabric for binding
- ¾ yard of backing fabric
- 26" x 32" piece of batting
- Black embroidery floss
- 1 red pom-pom

Cutting

All measurements include ¼"-wide seam allowance.

From the striped fabric, cut:
- 1 rectangle, 7½" x 11½"

From the polka-dot fabric, cut:
- 2 rectangles, 5½" x 7½"
- 1 strip, 1½" x 21½"

From *each* of the 9 prints, cut:
- 1 strip, 3½" x 42"; crosscut into 5 squares, 3½" x 3½" (45 squares total; you will use 42)

From the red print, cut:
- 1 strip, 2½" x 21½"

From the red-and-white fabric, cut:
- 3 strips, 2" x 42"

Now this is the ultimate security blanket! The sleepy sock monkey is all settled in to slumber under his own security blanket too. Any kid on your list will be thrilled to receive this one-of-a-kind quilt!

Assembling the Background

1. Sew the striped rectangle between the two 5½" x 7½" polka-dot rectangles. Press the seams toward the polka-dot fabric.

2. Sew the 21½" polka-dot strip to the top of the unit from step 1. Press the seam toward the strip.

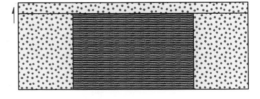

Appliquéing the Monkey

The monkey was appliquéd using the freezer-paper method. You can use your favorite technique. Refer to "Appliquéing" on page 86 for detailed instructions.

1. Trace the pattern shapes on pages 84 and 85. Cut the monkey shapes from the brown and cream scraps, a bow from the polka-dot scrap, and a mouth from the red scrap. You may appliqué a red circle on top of the hat if you do not wish to add a pom-pom.

2. Center the prepared appliqué shapes on the middle of the pillow background as shown. Baste or pin in place. Appliqué each piece in numerical order as shown on the patterns. Add the arm and bow appliqués after the quilt top is assembled.

3. Appliqué the eyes using a black scrap or embroider them with black floss. Stem stitch the eyelashes, nose, and mouth and ear details with two strands of embroidery floss.

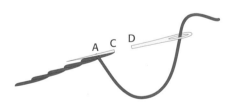

Stem stitch

Piecing the Monkey's "Quilt"

Arrange the assorted 3½" squares into six rows of seven squares each. Sew the squares together into rows; press the seams in opposite directions from row to row. Sew the rows together and press.

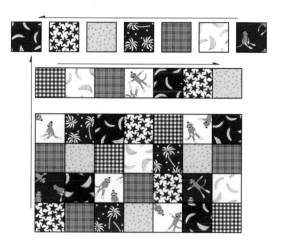

Assembling the Quilt

1. Sew the red strip between the top appliqué piece and the pieced squares. Press the seams toward the strip.

2. Finish appliquéing the monkey by adding the arms to both sides and the bow around his neck. Stem stitch the bow details with two strands of embroidery floss.

Quilt diagram

Finishing Your Quilt

Refer to "General Directions" on page 86 for specific directions regarding each of the following steps.

1. Layer the quilt top with the backing and batting; baste.

2. Hand or machine quilt as desired. My suggestions include quilting the blocks in the ditch and outline quilting around the appliqué.

3. Trim the batting and backing even with the quilt-top edges.

4. Referring to "Straight-Cut Binding" on page 94, prepare the red-and-white strips for binding and sew the binding to the quilt.

5. Hand sew the red pom-pom to the top of the monkey's hat. Needle up and down through the quilt and pom-pom four to five times, knotting at the beginning and end to securely attach the pom-pom to the quilt.

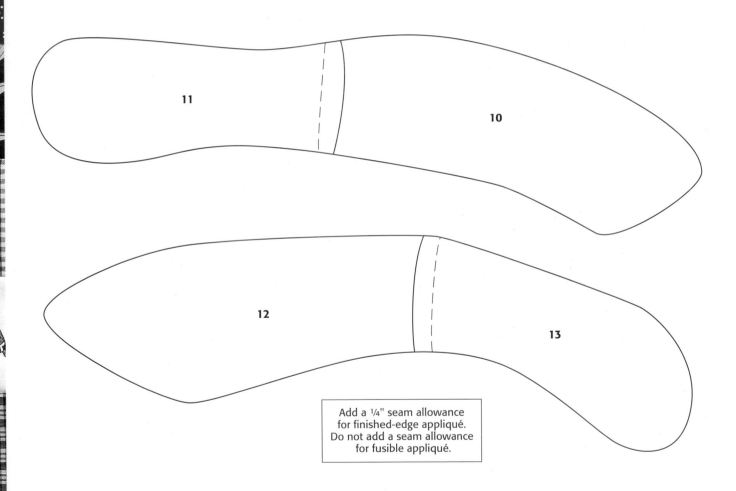

Add a ¼" seam allowance
for finished-edge appliqué.
Do not add a seam allowance
for fusible appliqué.

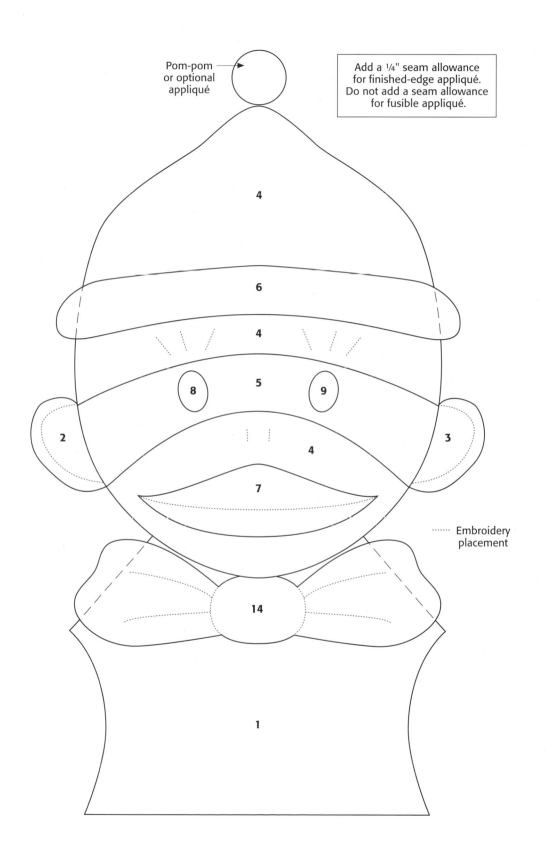

Pom-pom
or optional
appliqué

Add a ¼" seam allowance
for finished-edge appliqué.
Do not add a seam allowance
for fusible appliqué.

4

6

4

8   5   9

2   3

4

7

Embroidery
placement

14

1

General Directions

This chapter includes helpful instructions for completing the projects in this book. To make sure that you are pleased with your finished quilt, sew accurate ¼"-wide seam allowances and follow the pressing directions with each step before proceeding to the next one.

Appliquéing

Instructions follow for three appliqué methods: freezer paper, needle turn, and fusible. The term *finished-edge appliqué* refers to an appliqué piece with a seam allowance added that is then turned under before that piece is appliquéd. Freezer paper and needle turn are finished-edge appliqué methods.

Freezer-Paper Appliqué

A freezer-paper template stabilizes the appliqué piece during the entire process. You can easily remove the freezer paper by cutting away the backing fabric behind the completed appliqué.

1. Trace the appliqué patterns on the unwaxed (dull) side of the freezer paper. If the patterns are directional or asymmetrical, reverse them. Cut out the templates on the traced lines.

2. Place the freezer-paper template, shiny side down, on the wrong side of the chosen fabric and use a dry iron to attach it to the fabric. Leave at least ¾" of space between pieces when attaching more than one freezer-paper template to the same fabric.

3. Cut out each shape, adding a ¼" seam allowance beyond the template edges. Trim the seam allowances to ³⁄₁₆" after cutting out each shape. Clip inner curves and trim points to eliminate bulk.

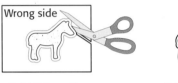

Cut ¼" from the freezer paper.

Trim the seam allowance to ³⁄₁₆".

4. Turn the seam allowances over the freezer-paper edge and secure with hand basting through the paper and both fabric layers.

5. Pin or baste the appliqué on the background fabric and sew it in place with an appliqué stitch (see "Hand-Appliqué Stitch" on page 88). Remove the basting.

6. On the wrong side of the appliqué piece, cut away the background fabric, leaving a ¼" seam allowance all around. Remove the freezer paper, using your fingers, a needle, or tweezers to gently pull it away from the appliqué.

Needle-Turn Appliqué

This is the most traditional and perhaps the most time-consuming appliqué method. If you love handwork, this is the method for you.

1. Trace the appliqué patterns on the unwaxed (dull) side of the freezer paper. Cut out the templates on the traced lines.

2. Place the freezer-paper templates, shiny side down, on the right side of the chosen fabric and use a dry iron to attach them to the fabric. Leave at least ¾" of space between pieces when attaching more than one freezer-paper template to the same fabric.

3. Use a No. 2 pencil on light fabric or use a white or yellow pencil on dark fabric to trace around each template.

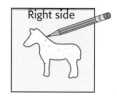

Trace around the freezer-paper template.

4. Cut out the appliqués, adding a scant ¼" seam allowance all around. Peel away the appliqué templates from each piece.

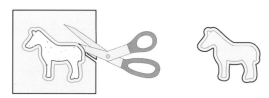

Cut with a ¼" seam allowance.

5. Position the appliqués on the background fabric and pin or baste in place.

6. Starting at a straight area on one edge of each appliqué, use the tip of the needle to turn under the allowances along the marked line, about ½" at a time. Clip the seam allowance as needed in curved areas. Sew in place with the hand-appliqué stitch (see "Hand-Appliqué Stitch" on page 88).

Clip curves up to the fold line.

Fusible Appliqué

This is the quickest appliqué method. Pieces are cut without turn-under seam allowances and are simply fused to the background. You can then stitch around the appliqués to make them durable for machine washing or leave the raw edges exposed for a quick and easy project.

1. Place fusible web, transfer-paper side up, on top of the appliqué pattern and trace the lines. If the pattern is directional or asymmetrical, it must be reversed. Group all pieces that will be cut from the same fabric with about ¼" of space between them. Cut around the group of appliqué templates.

2. Place the fusible web on the wrong side of the appropriate fabric, paper side up, and fuse following the manufacturer's directions.

3. Cut out the pieces on the traced lines and peel away the paper backing. Position the appliqués, right side up, on the background and fuse in place following the manufacturer's directions.

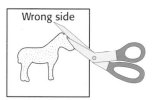

Cut along the edge of the fusible web.

Hand-Appliqué Stitch

Choose a long, thin needle, such as a Sharp, for stitching.

1. Tie a knot in a single strand of thread that closely matches the appliqué color.

2. From the wrong side of the appliqué, bring the needle up on the fold line and blind stitch along the folded edge. Take a stitch about every ⅛".

Appliqué stitch

3. To end your stitching, pull the needle through to the wrong side. Take two small stitches, making knots by taking your needle through the loops.

Machine-Appliqué Stitch

"Zoo Polka" and "Pocket Quilt" were both machine appliquéd. Using matching thread and a satin stitch makes an attractive edge that is very durable.

1. Attach an open-toe appliqué foot so you can see the needle without the foot obscuring your view.

2. Thread your machine with a lightweight (60-weight) embroidery thread. Set your machine for a narrow zigzag stitch and stitch completely around the appliqué shape.

Invisible Machine-Appliqué Stitch

Machine stitches that can be used for invisible machine appliqué will vary with the make and model of the machine used. The trick is to try to mimic the hand appliqué stitch using your machine.

1. Thread the top of your machine with invisible nylon monofilament thread. In the bobbin, use cotton thread or cotton-covered polyester thread to match the background fabric.

2. Attach an open-toe appliqué foot.

3. For the most basic sewing machine, use a zigzag stitch 1 mm to 1.5 mm long and about 1 mm wide. The blind hem stitch is another stitch that works well if you are able to adjust the length and width of the stitch. You will need to practice a little with your machine and see what works best for you.

4. Place your appliqué piece under the pressure foot so that the left swing position of the needle will stitch into the appliqué and the right swing position will stitch into the background fabric.

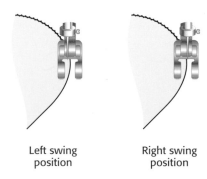

Left swing   Right swing
position   position

5. Stitch around the piece, overlapping the starting point by a few stitches to secure.

Circle Appliqués

The trick to a good circle appliqué is to prepare a precise template.

1. Use template plastic to trace the circle size you need. Cut out the template and write the size directly onto the template.

2. Trace the circle onto card stock or a manila folder. Cut out the circle. You can reuse the circle many times as long as it keeps its shape.

3. Place the card-stock circle on the appliqué fabric and cut around the template adding a generous ¼" seam allowance.

4. Thread a needle and tie a knot in the thread. Sew a small running stitch around the circle, ⅛" from the cut edge, beginning and ending in the right side of the fabric.

5. With the wrong side of the fabric facing up, place the card-stock template in the middle of the fabric. Pull the basting thread until it gathers around the circle. Tie off the thread securely.

6. Steam press around the edges of the circle. Use spray starch for a crisp edge. Snip the threads and remove the template.

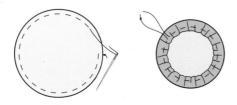

7. Appliqué the circle in place either by hand or machine using the invisible appliqué stitch.

Quick and Easy Flying Geese

The following method is an easy way to quickly make four flying-geese units at a time. Each unit is made up of two small squares from a background fabric and one large square that becomes the "goose" triangle (the large triangle in the middle).

1. On each of the smaller background squares, draw a light pencil line diagonally from corner to corner. To make it easier to mark the fabric, place the squares on the gritty side of a piece of very fine-grain sandpaper so they won't slip while you draw.

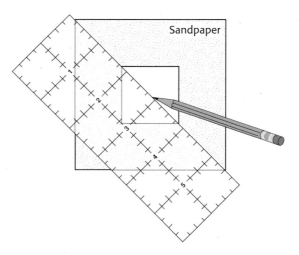

2. With right sides together, place the small background squares at opposite corners of the large square, aligning the edges. The background squares will slightly overlap in the center. Pin in place. Sew an accurate ¼" seam on each side of the drawn line.

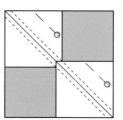

3. Cut the square in half diagonally on the drawn line. Flip the small triangles open and press the seams toward them.

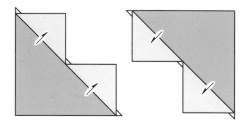

4. Position another small square in the corner of each of the two units from step 3 as shown. Sew an accurate ¼" seam on each side of the drawn line.

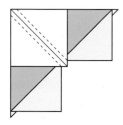

5. Cut on the pencil line to create two flying-geese units from each triangle. Press the seams toward the small triangle.

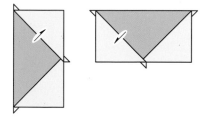

6. Repeat steps 1–5 to make the required number of flying-geese units for your project.

Adding Borders

This section describes the most basic directions for making borders.

Straight-Cut Borders

1. Measure the length of the quilt top through the center. Cut border strips to this measurement, piecing as necessary. Mark the center of the quilt edges and border strips. Pin the border strips to the sides of the quilt top, matching the center marks and ends and easing as necessary. Sew the border strips in place. Press the seams toward the border.

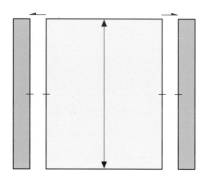

Measure the center of the quilt, top to bottom. Mark the centers.

2. Measure the width of the quilt top through the center, including the side-border strips just added. Cut border strips to this measurement, piecing as necessary. Mark the center of the quilt edges and the border strips. Pin the border strips to the top and bottom edges of the quilt top, matching the center marks and ends, and easing as necessary; stitch. Press the seams toward the border.

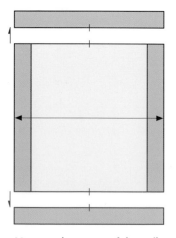

Measure the center of the quilt, side to side, including the borders. Mark the centers.

Mitered Borders

Strips for mitered borders are cut extra long and trimmed to fit after stitching the mitered corners. If your quilt has more than one border, you can sew all the border strips together for each side first and then sew them all to the quilt top at once. When you are mitering the corners, be sure to match the seam intersections of each different border.

1. To add a border with mitered corners, measure the quilt top through the center in both directions and mark the appropriate measurement on the top border strip with a pin at each end. Pin-mark the center of the strip. Pin the strip to the top edge, matching the center to the quilt-top center and aligning the pins at each end. An even amount of excess border strip should extend beyond each end of the quilt top.

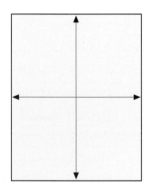

2. Stitch, beginning and ending the seam ¼" from the quilt-top corners. Repeat with the remaining border strips.

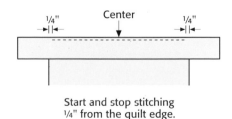

Start and stop stitching
¼" from the quilt edge.

3. Working on a flat surface, place one border on top of the other at a 90° angle.

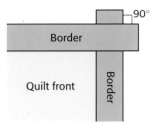

4. Fold the top border layer back at a 45° angle and press to mark the stitching line.

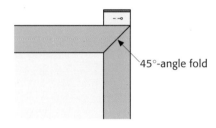

45°-angle fold

5. With right sides together, pin the borders together. Begin stitching at the inner corner, sewing on the crease and backstitching as you begin and end the stitching.

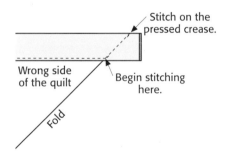

Stitch on the pressed crease.

Wrong side of the quilt

Begin stitching here.

Fold

6. Trim away the excess border fabric, leaving a ¼"-wide seam allowance. Press the seam open. Repeat with the remaining corners.

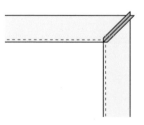

Trim the mitered seams
and press open.

Layering the Quilt

The quilt "sandwich" consists of the backing, batting, and quilt top. I recommend cutting the quilt backing at least 4" larger than the quilt top all around for the crib-sized quilts. The smaller doll and wall quilts need to be at least 2" larger all around. Many of the quilts in this book are just on the edge of needing an extra length of fabric for the backing. In this case I often piece some strips of coordinating fabrics to add a little interest to the back and save buying another length of fabric. Below are two arrangements that that work well for the back of a crib quilt. However, each project's materials list does state the full amount of yardage required to make a backing of all one fabric.

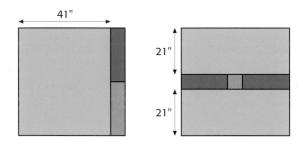

1. Spread the backing, wrong side up, on a flat, clean surface. Anchor it with pins or masking tape. Be careful not to stretch the backing out of shape.

2. Spread the batting over the backing, smoothing out any wrinkles.

3. Place the pressed quilt top, right side up, on top of the batting. Smooth out any wrinkles and make sure the edges of the quilt top are parallel to the edges of the backing.

4. For hand quilting, start in the center and hand baste the layers together in a grid of horizontal and vertical lines spaced 6" to 8" apart. Baste around the outer edges of the quilt top.

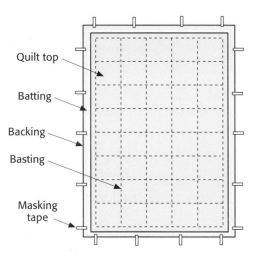

Quilt top
Batting
Backing
Basting
Masking tape

For machine quilting, pin the layers together using #1 nickel-plated safety pins. Begin pinning the center, working toward the outside edges and placing pins every 3" to 4" throughout.

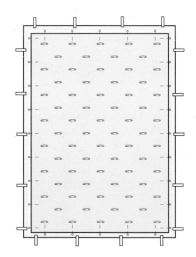

Quilting

All the quilts in this book were machine quilted. "Boxed Dots," "Flannel Blocks with Polka Dots," and "Mr. Lucky" were professionally machine quilted by Nona King. I like to machine quilt kids' quilts because they are an easy size to fit under the sewing machine, and I think it also adds to their durability.

For straight-line quilting, it is extremely helpful to have a walking foot to feed the quilt layers through the machine without shifting or puckering. Some machines have a built-in walking foot or even-feed feature; other machines require a separate attachment.

Walking foot

Use free-motion quilting to outline a quilt pattern in the fabric or to create stippling and other curved designs. You will need a darning foot and the ability to drop the feed dogs on your machine. Instead of turning the fabric to change directions, you guide the fabric in the direction of the design, using the needle like a pencil.

Darning foot

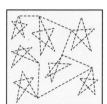
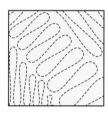

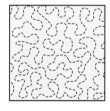

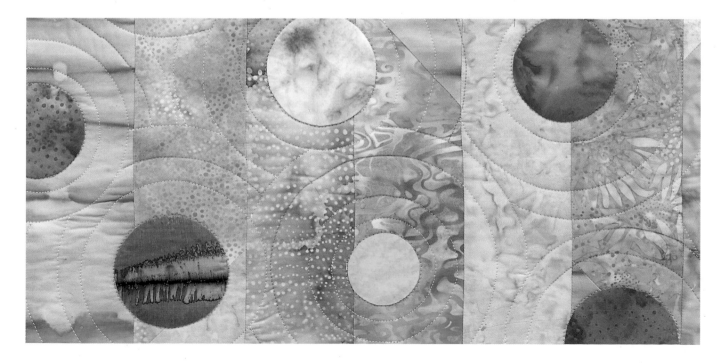

Binding

Binding finishes the edges of your quilt. I prefer using a double-fold binding for its durability. Most binding strips are cut across the fabric width and are referred to as *straight-cut binding*. I also like the look of stripes, plaids, and checks cut on the bias, referred to as *bias-cut binding*. This is the same method as straight-cut binding, except the strips are cut on the bias in-stead of across the grain.

Straight-Cut Binding

To make straight-cut, double-layer binding, also known as French binding, cut crosswise strips, 2" wide. You will need enough strips to go around the perimeter of the quilt plus 10" for the seams and corners in the mitered folds.

1. With right sides together, sew the strips together on the diagonal as shown to create one long strip. Trim the excess fabric and press the seams open.

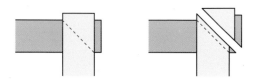

2. Cut one end at a 45° angle. Turn this end under ¼" and press. Fold the strip in half lengthwise, wrong sides together, and press.

Fold line

3. Trim the batting and the backing even with the quilt-top edges, making sure the corners are square.

4. Beginning on one edge of the quilt and using a ¼"-wide seam allowance, start sewing about 3" from the beginning of the binding. Keep the raw edges even with the quilt-top edge. End the stitching ¼" from the corner of the quilt and backstitch.

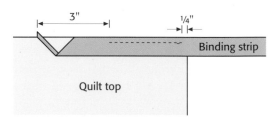

3"   ¼"

Binding strip

Quilt top

5. Turn the quilt so that you will be stitching down the next side. Fold the binding up, away from the quilt and then back down onto itself, aligning the raw edges with the quilt-top edge. Begin stitching at the edge, backstitching to secure, and end ¼" from the lower edge. Repeat on the remaining edges.

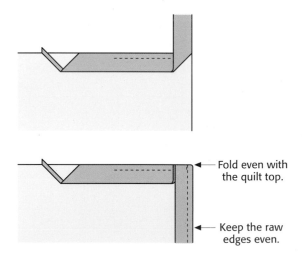

← Fold even with the quilt top.

← Keep the raw edges even.

6. When you reach the beginning of the binding, lap the end of the binding strip over the beginning by about 1" and cut away any excess binding. Trim the end at a 45° angle. Tuck the end of the binding into the fold and complete the seam.

7. Fold the binding over the raw edges of the quilt to the back, with the folded edge just covering the machine stitching. Blind stitch in place, including the miter that forms at each corner.

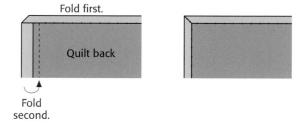

Bias-Cut Binding

Plaid and striped fabrics look especially dramatic for binding or to cover cording when cut on the bias.

1. Place a ruler with the 45°-angle marking along the bottom edge of a single layer of fabric that has been placed on your rotary mat. Cut along the length of the ruler.

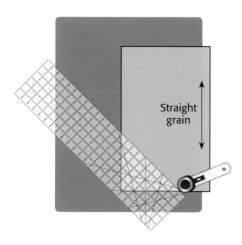

2. Measuring from the bias edge you just made, cut as many bias strips as needed, at the width specified, for the quilt you are making.

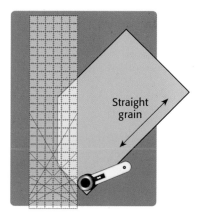

3. With right sides together, place bias-cut strips on a diagonal and sew across the strips as shown. Press the seams open.

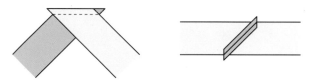

4. Be sure one end is cut at a 45° angle. Turn this end under ¼" and press. Fold the strips in half lengthwise, wrong side together, and press.

5. Follow steps 3–7 in "Straight-Cut Binding" starting on page 94 to attach the binding strip to the quilt.

About the Author

Jean Van Bockel started quilting in 1986 when she joined a quilt group in Snohomish, Washington. She feels fortunate to have learned from so many accomplished quilters over the years and attributes much of her skill and knowledge to her current quilt group, the Out to Lunch Bunch.

Jean has taught beginning quilting and hand-appliqué classes, and is well known for her creative designs and award-winning quilts.

She has written two other books published by Martingale & Company: *Quilts from Larkspur Farm*, with Pam Mostek, and *Meadowbrook Quilts*.

Jean and her husband, Mark, have lived in northern Idaho for the past 15 years. They are the parents of three grown children. Jean enjoys daily walks with their two dogs, Foster and Cedar.